序

早在神農氏時代，中國人嚐百草發現了茶，到宋朝時代更將「茶」發揚光大，除了加強茶味的芬芳外，更出現了千奇百樣的附庸品－－飲茶點心。

而在中國各省裡，廣東人把「飲茶」與「點心」融合的最澈底，他們將它當成正餐，以一款一款的小點心，與依各人喜愛的烏龍茶、香片、龍井、鐵觀音、清茶……搭配，成為世界聞名的「ㄢ茶」。

昔日在農業社會階段，人們在工作後閒來無事，便喜歡ㄠ喝親朋好友到茶館裡閒嗑牙，在品茗之餘，叫幾道小點增加飲茶豐富性。所以，每道廣式點心的數量都不多，以小蒸籠、小碟、中盤上桌。這種飲茶習慣沿襲至今，現代人雖然不再至茶館裡消磨終日，但是仍對這種悠閒、自在的茗酌方式趨之若鶩。

在台灣茶樓林立的現況下，繁忙的人們常把ㄢ茶當作早午合一餐，邀約至親好友餐敘，在無拘無束的飲茶氣氛中，情感水乳交融；更有工商界人士利用ㄢ茶時談生意，在輕鬆、自在的交談裡達成交易，也解決了吃飯問題。

特殊的是，台灣目前的飲茶餐館裡，除了以「廣東點心」為主外，並兼容並蓄地加入一些台式口味、江浙小品、平津小點……等，拓展飲茶點心的範疇，使喜歡飲茶的消費層面愈見愈廣。

除了中國人外，英國人也講究喝茶。他們常在下午挪出一段空檔，定之為「飲茶時間」。或是獨自品茗，或是邀友談心，以提振精神，紓解壓力。現在台灣也有流行喝咖啡吃點心的趨勢，使「飲茶點心」更延伸觸角成為「咖啡點心」。

針對各式點心需求量的日益蓬勃，味全家政班張鴻欽老師和同仁們精心策劃了這本「飲茶食譜」。以八個月的收集資料、研究改進、烹調製作……，出版了這本共有八十八道點心的精緻好書。

書中，除了詳細介紹各類點心的製作過程外，並有小圖片的示範動作。在書前以圖示介紹各種材料及發麵技巧。讀者們只要依照書中作法，即可調理出如餐館中一樣的可口點心，而自製飲茶點心，除了可以避免油膩、保持衛生外，更能邀約孩子、家人一起料理、共同品嚐，達到寓教於樂、品嚐佳餚、親子溝通……等多重效果。

「飲茶食譜」是一本持家烹飪、創業的好書，八十八道的各種風味點心，定會獲得大家的肯定。

Preface

The custom of tea drinking in China dates back to the legendary Shen Nung, who is said to have personally tried hundreds of grasses and herbs to test their medicinal effects and toxicity. Tea was a widely popular drink by the Sung Dynasty (960-1280 A.D.), and gradually, innovations in the tea drinking custom were introduced. In addition to a high level of connoisseurship of the various types of teas and improvements in the quality of tea leaves, a broad variety of accompaniments to tea drinking began to appear—dim sum.

Among China's provinces, "dim sum" and "tea drinking" are most closely interlinked in Kwangtung Province, where dim sum and tea can comprise an entire meal. In the Cantonese *yum cha* ("tea drinking") ritual, varieties of dim sum are served one after the other, along with one's favorite tea, be it Oolong, Jasmine, Dragon Well, Iron Buddha, or green tea.

In China's ancient agricultural society, people would often head for tea houses after an exhausting day in the fields. Here they would mix warm conversation with fine tea and a tantalizing selection of dim sum. The quantity of each was kept small—the delicacies were served in tiers of bamboo steamers or small to medium-sized plates—so that many different varieties could be sampled. This custom has continued up through the present day. Although people no longer while away entire days in tea houses, the leisurely tea drinking custom is still a frequent and favored activity.

In Taiwan, which boasts more than a few tea houses, *yum cha* is often a mid-morning brunch that takes care of both breakfast and lunch in one meal. Close friends and family are often invited along for a time to let down the usual weekday barriers and enjoy unrestrained conversation. Business people often like to strike deals over a relaxed mid-morning *yum cha* brunch.

A unique feature of Taiwan's tea houses is that, in addition to the usual run of Cantonese-style dim sum, you will find culinary specialties of Taiwan, Kiangsu and Chekiang provinces, the Peking and Tientsin areas, and other regions of China. This broadens the concept and experience of dim sum, and provides a greater variety from which to choose.

The British are famous for their custom of "afternoon tea," a time during which they push aside the pressing matters of the day to relax and enjoy good tea or coffee and pastries, either alone or with family and friends. The custom of coffee drinking has also gradually caught on in Taiwan, so that today, a plate of dim sum may just as well turn up next to a cup of Brazilian coffee as Chinese tea.

In response to the ever-growing popularity of the various regional styles of dim sum, Master Chef Chang Hung-chin and his colleagues at Wei-Chuan's Cooking School in Taipei put painstaking efforts into preparing this book of *Chinese Dim Sum*. Over a period of eight months, they collected materials and information from every possible source, then studied and carefully improved upon each recipe. They tested and retested each one until everyone in the group was satisfied that it was as perfect as they could make it. The result is this superb collection of 88 recipes for making professional quality dim sum in your own kitchen.

This book gives detailed, step-by-step descriptions of how to make each individual type of dim sum, and further clarifies more difficult steps through abundant illustrations. Special ingredients and instructions for making the various kinds of doughs are featured at the beginning of the book. All you have to do is follow this book, step by step, and you will turn out dim sum snacks able to compete with those served at the finest tea houses. And since you made them yourself, you know that they contain only the best and purest ingredients. Have the children share in the preparation and let them learn while they have fun. They—and the rest of the family—will enjoy the final results even more because of their personal involvement in the preparation.

Chinese Dim Sum can help you either at home or in professional cooking with its 88 distinctive types of dim sum. It is sure to win the hearts and palates of all who experience what it has to offer.

Lee Hwa Lin

麵皮種類
Types of Dough

醱麵：
在麵點的製作過程中，利用酵母菌的分解而使得麵糰組織變得鬆軟並膨脹即為醱麵。

Yeast dough:
Dough in which yeast is used to make the dough light and airy.

燙麵：
麵粉加高溫熱水揉成的麵糰稱為燙麵，又名死麵。燙麵可塑性高、不變形，再加熱後質地較冷水麵柔軟，常用於蒸餃燒賣之類的外皮。

Hot water dough:
Dough made with hot water has greater elasticity and holds its shape better. After cooking, hot water dough comes out somewhat softer than dough made with cold water. Hot water dough is often used in making the outer wrappers for steamed dumplings and siu mai.

半燙麵：

燙麵、冷水麵以一比一的份量揉合的麵糰稱之。具兩者之特性，常用在煎類的點心外皮上。

Combination dough:

Dough made from a combination of half hot water dough and half cold water dough possesses the characteristics of both types of dough, and is often used in flour wrappers for pan-fried dim sum.

冷水麵：

麵粉加常溫的水所揉成的麵糰稱為冷水麵，再加熱後質地較具韌性，最常用於水餃皮的製作。

Cold water dough:

After cooking, dough made with tepid (room temperature) water comes out somewhat firmer than hot water dough. It is often used to make dumpling wrappers.

薑米醋：

以薑末２大匙、白醋２大匙、冷開水２大匙、鹽少許、糖 $\frac{1}{4}$ 小匙、香油 $\frac{1}{4}$ 小匙、醬油 $\frac{1}{4}$ 小匙等調勻而成。常作餃子或海鮮類食品的沾料，既可增加風味，又可降低對海鮮的過敏。

Ginger vinegar:

Ginger vinegar is made by combining 2 tablespoons finely minced ginger root with 2 tablespoons white rice vinegar, 2 tablespoons water, a pinch of salt, ¼ teaspoon sugar, ¼ teaspoon sesame oil, and ¼ teaspoon soy sauce. This is often used as a dip for dumplings or seafood; it both adds flavor and reduces any fishy flavor.

①篩子　Sieve
②秤子　Scale
③量匙　Measuring spoons
④麵刀　Dough knife
⑤抹刀　Spreading knife
⑥量杯　Measuring cup

使用工具
Utensils

⑦刷子　Brush
⑧刮刀　Rubber spatula
⑨捏麵棍(擀杖)
　　Chinese rolling pin
⑩烤模(蛋塔、椰子塔)
　　Tart molds
　　(for Custard Tarts
　　and Coconut Tarts)
⑪打蛋器　Egg whisk

一般材料　Basic Ingredients

①髮菜　Hair seaweed
②春捲皮　Spring roll wrappers
（潤餅皮）　(lumpia wrappers)
③臘腸　Chinese sausage
④葱白　Green onion (white portion)
⑤鹹蛋黃　Salt-preserved egg yolk
⑥油葱酥　Fried green onion flakes
⑦大蒜　Fresh garlic
⑧蝦米　Dried shrimps
⑨紅葱頭　Shallots

⑩豆腐皮　Bean curd skin
⑪韮黃　Yellow Chinese chives
⑫香菜　Fresh coriander
⑬玉米醬　Cream style corn
⑭在來米　Long grain rice
⑮沙蝦　Raw shrimp
⑯花枝肉　Squid fillet
⑰栗子　Chestnuts
⑱蓬萊米　Short grain rice

特殊材料

特殊材料	主要成份	用　　途	購買地點	儲存方式
① 乾澄粉	脫筋後的麵粉	糯米球、水晶餃的皮	AC	♥
② 蠔油	鮮蝦、鹽、水、糖、澱粉、醬色	炒餡料、炒菜	AB	■
③ 在來米粉	在來米	碗粿、蘿蔔糕	ABC	♥●
④ 熟黑白芝蔴粉	黑、白芝蔴炒黃並碾碎	沾料	E	♥
⑤ 鮮味露	脫水性植物性蛋白質、鹽	炒餡料、炒菜	AB	—
⑥ 味噌	黃豆	沾料、作湯	ABI	■★
⑦ 酥油	植物油氫化而成	西點點心	D	●
⑧ 奶油	牛脂肪提煉	點心	ADH	▲
⑨ 奶水	鮮奶濃縮	點心、菜餚	ABC	■★
⑩ 煉乳	鮮奶、糖加工濃縮	點心、菜餚	AB	■★
⑪ 白醬油	黃豆釀造	作菜	AB	■●
⑫ 肥板油	猪肚與內臟間的油脂	炸油、內餡	AF	◆★
⑬ 軟凍粉	玉米澱粉、香料等	點心之皮或餡	D	♥
⑭ 香草片	香草	香味來源	AD	♥

特殊材料	主要成份	用　　途	購買地點	儲存方式
⑮ 花生油	花生壓榨之油脂	炒菜	AB	♥●
⑯ 豆沙	紅豆—黑豆沙 花生—白豆沙	點心餡料	DH	▲
⑰ 蓮蓉	蓮子	點心餡料	DH	▲
⑱ 棗泥	黑棗	點心餡料	DH	▲
⑲ 硬肥肉	肥猪肉	炸油、內餡	AF	★
⑳ 香油	芝蔴提煉之油脂	作菜、湯	AB	♥●
㉑ 中筋麵粉	小麥	發麵類食品	AB	♥●
㉒ 玉米粉	玉米	內餡勾芡	AB	♥●
㉓ 花生粉	花生	內餡、沾料	A	♥★
㉔ 桂花醬	桂花醃製而成	作點心、菜餚	AG	♥●
㉕ 椰子粉	椰子	點心內餡、外皮沾裏	ABCD	♥●
㉖ 黃色5號	食用色素	點心等顏色加深	D	♥
㉗ 酵母	酵母	發麵	AB	♥*
㉘ 熟麵粉	麵粉炒熟	作牛舌餅、椒鹽芝蔴酥、花生酥餅	E	♥

Special Ingredients

	Special Ingredient	Main Ingredients	Uses	Where Sold	How to Store
1	(dry) wheat starch	deglutenized flour	glutinous rice balls, crystal dumplings	A B C	♥
2	oyster sauce	fresh oysters, salt, water, sugar, starch, caramel color	fillings, stir-frys	A B	■
3	long grain rice flour	long grain rice	rice bowl mold, radish cake	A B C	♥ ●
4	white (black) sesame seed, toasted and ground into a powder	white (black) sesame seed	dips	E	♥
5	Maggi sauce	dehydrated vegetable protein, salt	fillings, stir-frys	A B D	—
6	miso	soy beans	dips, soups	A B D I	■ ★
7	shortening	hydrogenated vegetable oil	Western style pastries	A D	●
8	butter	milk fat	dim sum	A H	▲
9	evaporated milk	milk with some water removed	dim sum, other dishes	A	■ ★
10	sweetened condensed milk	condensed milk + sugar	dim sum, other dishes	A	■ ★
11	light-colored soy sauce	fermented soy beans	general use	A B D	■ ●
12	leaf lard	fat from pork stomach and internal organs	deep frying, fillings	A F	★ ◆
13	Custard Powder	Cornstarch、flavour	dim sum doughs and fillings	B D	♥
14	vanilla extract	vanilla bean, alcohol	flavoring	A D	♥
15	peanut oil	oil extracted from peanuts	stir-frys	A B D	♥ ●
16	sweet red bean paste	red (adzuki) beans or kidney beans	dim sum fillings	B D	▲
17	lotus seed paste	lotus seeds	dim sum fillings	B D	▲
18	Chinese date paste	black Chinese dates	dim sum fillings	B D	▲
19	fat pork	pork fat	deep frying, fillings	A F	★
20	sesame oil	oil pressed from sesame seeds	various dishes, soups	A B D	♥ ●
21	all-purpose (medium gluten) flour	wheat	yeast doughs	A	♥ ●
22	cornstarch	corn	thickening fillings	A	♥ ●
23	peanut powder	peanuts	fillings and coatings	A B	♥ ★
24	sweet osmanthus jam	pickled osmanthus blossoms	dim sum, other dishes	B G	♥ ●
25	desiccated coconut	coconut	fillings, coatings	A B C D	♥ ●
26	food coloring	food dye	coloring	A	♥
27	active dry yeast	yeast	rising dough	A	♥ ✳
28	roasted flour	flour roasted in a dry wok	used in some fillings	E	♥

購買地點 Where to buy ingredients:

A. 超市   A. Supermarket
B. 雜貨店   B. Oriental grocery
C. 迪化街   C. Tihua Street, Taipei
D. 食品材料行   D. Food specialty store
E. 自製   E. Make it yourself
F. 肉販   F. Butcher
G. 中藥行   G. Chinese pharmacy
H. 麵包店   H. Bakery
I. 醬菜店   I. Pickled foods shop

儲存方式   How to store: Key to symbols used

■ 勿沾水，以防發霉   ■ Avoid contact with water to prevent mold from forming.
★ 冷藏   ★ Refrigerate.
♥ 保持乾燥   ♥ Keep dry.
● 通風陰涼處   ● Keep in a cool, ventilated place.
✳ 勿冷凍   ✳ Do not freeze.
▲ 應冷凍   ▲ Freeze.
◆ 上有一層膜要撕掉   ◆ Remove the top membrane.

目錄 Contents

發麵類 Yeast Dough Dim Sum

燙麵類 Hot Water Dough Dim Sum

酥皮類 Flaky Dough Pastries

糕粿類 Cakes and Mochi

其他類 Miscellaneous

承蒙好望角畫廊、陸羽茶藝、人間茶藝等提供道具，謹此致謝。

With many thanks to the Cape of Good Hope Gallery, the Lu Yu Teahouse, and the Jenchien Teahouse for providing settings for the photographs.

1 豆沙小包：作法見第14頁　Red Bean Paste Buns (P.14)
2 芋泥小包：作法見第15頁　Taro Paste Buns (P.15)
3 水晶小包：作法見第15頁　Crystal Buns (P.15)
4 芝蔴小包：作法見第16頁　Sweet Sesame Buns (P.16)
5 椰蓉小包：作法見第16頁　Coconut Buns (P.16)

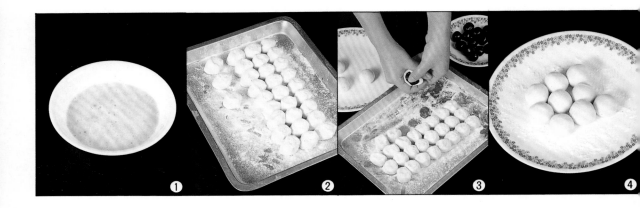

豆沙小包

Red Bean Paste Buns

材料：
外皮：

中筋麵粉	300公克
糖	37.5公克
猪油	1大匙
泡打粉	1小匙
香草粉	$\frac{1}{2}$小匙
水	150公克
酵母	11公克

內餡：豆沙 …………… 300公克

❶外皮：酵母溶於水(圖1)，和其它材料拌匀揉成麵
　糰，再分割30個小麵粒(圖2)。
❷豆沙分成30等份。
❸將豆沙入小麵糰中(圖3)，並放置醒40分鐘(圖4)
　，再移入蒸籠中大火蒸5分鐘即可。
■靜置等待發酵的過程稱「醒」。

INGREDIENTS:
Dough:

300g (²⁄₃ lb.)	all-purpose (medium gluten) flour
37.5g (1¹⁄₃ oz.)	sugar
1 T.	lard or shortening
1 t.	baking powder
½ t.	vanilla extract
150g (¹⁄₃ lb.)	water
11g (½ oz.)	active dry yeast

Filling:

300g (²⁄₃ lb.)	sweet red bean paste

❶ Dough: Dissolve the yeast in the water (illus. 1). Mix into the other dough ingredients and knead until smooth. Divide the dough into 30 equally sized portions (illus. 2).
❷ Divide the red bean paste into 30 equally sized portions.
❸ Wrap one portion of red bean paste inside each portion of dough (illus. 3). Allow to rise 40 minutes (illus. 4). Arrange in a steamer and steam over high heat for 5 minutes.

芋泥小包

材料：
外皮：與豆沙小包相同（見第14頁）
內餡：

去皮芋頭 ……300公克	糯米粉（圖1）……75公克
細糖 ………150公克	雞蛋 ………………1個
熟豬油 ………75公克	

❶芋頭切片蒸熟，趁熱搗碎（圖2），待涼後加入其他材料拌勻即為內餡。

❷每份外皮包入1大匙內餡（圖3），放置醒40分鐘，再入蒸鍋大火蒸6分鐘即可。

■若餡太粘，可稍冷凍，使其凝結（圖4）。

Taro Paste Buns

INGREDIENTS:
Dough: Same as for Red Bean Paste Buns (p. 14).

Filling:
300g (2/3 lb.)	taros, pared
150g (1/3 lb.)	sugar
75g (2½ oz.)	lard (cooked)
75g (2½ oz.)	glutinous (mochi) flour (illus. 1)
1	egg

❶ Slice the pared taros and steam until soft. Mash while hot (illus. 2). Allow to cool, and then mix in the rest of the ingredients until well blended to form the filling.

❷ Wrap 1 tablespoon of filling in each portion of dough (illus. 3). Allow to rise for 40 minutes. Arrange in a steamer and steam over high heat for 6 minutes.

■ If the filling is too sticky, it can be partially frozen to make it easier to handle (illus. 4).

水晶小包

材料：
外皮：與豆沙小包相同（見第14頁）
內餡：

絞碎肥板油（圖1）……	細糖………………75公克
………225公克	葡萄乾…………75公克
桔餅…………75公克	熟白芝蔴………37公克
冬瓜糖…………75公克	

❶桔餅、多瓜糖切碎（圖2）和其它材料拌勻成內餡（圖3）。

❷每份外皮包入1大匙內餡（圖4），並放置醒40分鐘，再入蒸鍋大火蒸6分鐘即可。

Crystal Buns

INGREDIENTS:
Dough: Same as for Red Bean Paste Buns (p. 14).

Filling:
225g (½ lb.)	ground leaf lard (illus. 1)
75g (2½ oz.)	candied kumquats
75g (2½ oz.)	wintermelon candy
75g (2½ oz.)	sugar
75g (2½ oz.)	raisins
37g (1⅓ oz.)	toasted white sesame seeds

❶ Mince the candied kumquats and wintermelon candy (illus. 2). Mix into the other ingredients until well combined to form the filling (illus. 3).

❷ Wrap one tablespoon of filling in each portion of dough (illus. 4). Allow to rise for 40 minutes. Arrange in a steamer and steam over high heat for 6 minutes.

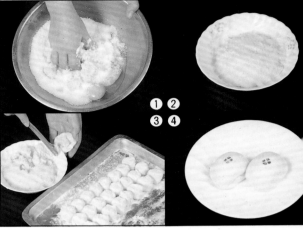

芝蔴小包

材料：
外皮：與豆沙小包相同（見第14頁）
內餡：

肥板油	………300公克	細糖	…………187公克
黑芝蔴粉	……150公克	熟豬油	…………75公克

❶肥板油剁細後（圖1），和其它材料拌勻即為芝蔴內餡（圖2）。
❷每份外皮包½大匙芝蔴餡（圖3），並放置醒40分鐘，再放入蒸鍋（圖4），大火蒸5分鐘即可。
■「熟豬油」即一般炸好的豬油。

Sweet Sesame Buns

INGREDIENTS:
Dough: Same as for Red Bean Paste Buns (p. 14).

Filling:
300g (⅔ lb.)   leaf lard
187g (6½ oz.)   sugar
150g (⅓ lb.)   black sesame powder
75g (2½ oz.)   lard (cooked)

❶ Mince the leaf lard finely (illus. 1) and combine with the other ingredients to make the sesame filling (illus. 2).
❷ Fill each portion of dough with ½ tablespoon of the sesame filling (illus. 3). Allow to rise 40 minutes. Arrange in a steamer (illus. 4) and steam over high heat for 5 minutes.

■ "Cooked lard" is obtained by frying pork fat.

椰蓉小包

材料：
外皮：與豆沙小包相同（見第14頁）
內餡：

椰子粉	………225公克	奶油	…………75公克
糖	…………150公克	鷄蛋	…………1個

❶將內餡材料揉勻後（圖1），略為冷凍使其凝結（圖2）。
❷每份外皮包入1小匙內餡（圖3），並放置醒40分鐘，再放入蒸籠中大火蒸5分鐘即可（圖4）。

Coconut Buns

INGREDIENTS:
Dough: Same as for Red Bean Paste Buns (p. 14).

Filling:
225g (½ lb.)   desiccated (or flaked) coconut
150g (⅓ lb.)   sugar (reduce sugar if using sweetened flaked coconut)
75g (2⅔ oz.)   butter
1   egg

❶ Mix the filling ingredients until well blended (illus. 1). Freeze until partially solid (illus. 2).
❷ Wrap one teaspoon of filling in each portion of dough (illus. 3). Allow to rise 40 minutes. Arrange in a steamer and steam over high heat for 5 minutes.

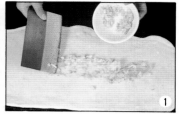

銀絲湘捲

材料：

外皮：

中筋麵粉 ······300公克
細糖 ··········37公克
泡打粉 ·······1小匙
沙拉油 ········1小匙
酵母 ·········15公克
水 ··········150公克

紅絲末·········少許

夾層油：

絞碎肥肉·······150公克
細糖 ·········75公克
香草片 ········4片

❶酵母溶於水後，與外皮其它材料揉成麵糰，提成30公分寬、0.5公分厚的薄皮。

❷夾層油先拌均勻。

❸將夾層油均勻地塗抹在薄麵皮上（圖1），折成3折（圖2），略爲整平後，用刀切成1.5公分寬的麵條捲成圓椎型（圖3），放置醒40分鐘。

❹用少許紅絲末裝飾在銀絲捲之頂端，續入蒸鍋大火蒸8分鐘即可。

Silver Thread Rolls

INGREDIENTS:

Dough:

300g (⅔ lb.)	all-purpose (medium gluten) flour
37g (1⅓ oz.)	sugar
1 t.	baking powder
1 t.	cooking oil
15g (½ oz.)	active dry yeast
150g (⅓ lb.)	water

Filling:

150g (⅓ lb.)	minced fat pork
75g (2⅔ oz.)	sugar
1 T.	vanilla extract

❶ Dissolve the yeast in the water, then mix with the other dough ingredients. Knead until smooth. Roll into a 30cm (12″) square to a thickness of about 0.5cm (¼″).

❷ Mix the filling ingredients until well combined and smooth.

❸ Spread the filling evenly over the dough (illus. 1), then fold the dough evenly into thirds (illus. 2). With a long knife or cleaver, cut the dough into strips about 1.5cm (¾″) wide. Roll each into a cone shape (illus. 3). Allow to rise 40 minutes.

❹ Garnish the tops of the silver thread rolls with minced candied fruit. Arrange in a steamer and steam over high heat for 8 minutes.

水煎包

Steam Fried Pork Rolls

材料：
外皮：

中筋麵粉 ……………………300公克
細糖 …………………………56公克
沙拉油 ………………………1大匙
泡打粉 ………………………1½小匙
水 ……………………………150公克
酵母 …………………………11公克

內餡：

高麗菜 ………………………300公克
絞肉 …………………………150公克
蝦皮 …………………………19公克
葱花 …………………………½杯
香油 …………………………3大匙
鹽 ……………………………1小匙
胡椒粉 ………………………1小匙
酒 ……………………………1小匙
味精 …………………………½小匙
沙拉油 ………………………1大匙
水 ……………………………1杯

❶酵母先溶於水後，再與外皮之其他材料揉勻，放置醒40分鐘。

❷高麗菜切碎，與內餡之其他材料拌勻即為內餡（圖1）。

❸醒過之麵糰略為搓揉後，分成25等份（圖2），每份包入1大匙內餡。

❹平底鍋先燒熱，入1大匙沙拉油，再把作好之包子排入澆入1杯水（圖3），蓋上鍋蓋，用中火燜煮10分鐘，待水乾後，續煎成兩面金黃即可。

INGREDIENTS:
Dough:

300g (²⁄₃ lb.)	all-purpose (medium gluten) flour
56g (2 oz.)	sugar
1 T.	cooking oil
1½ t.	baking powder
150g (⅓ lb.)	water
11g (½ oz.)	active dry yeast

Filling:

300g (²⁄₃ lb.)	cabbage
150g (⅓ lb.)	ground pork
19g (²⁄₃ oz.)	dried baby shrimp (hsia-p'i)
½ c.	chopped green onion
3 T.	sesame oil
1 t.	salt
1 t.	white pepper
1 t.	rice wine
1 T.	cooking oil
1 c.	water

❶ Dissolve the yeast in the water, then mix with the other dough ingredients until smooth. Allow to rise 40 minutes.

❷ Chop the cabbage finely and mix together with the other filling ingredients to form the filling (illus. 1).

❸ After the dough has risen, knead it lightly, then divide into 25 equally sized pieces (illus. 2). Wrap one tablespoon of filling in each piece of dough.

❹ Heat a frying pan, pour in one tablespoon cooking oil, then arrange the filled rolls in the pan. Add one cup of water (illus. 3), cover, then allow to cook over medium heat for about 10 minutes. After the water has boiled away, continue to fry the rolls until both sides are golden brown.

1 梅干肉包：作法見第22頁　Pork and Preserved Greens Buns (P.22)
2 滷肉包子：作法見第23頁　Soy-Stewed Pork Buns (P.23)
3 菜肉包子：作法見第24頁　Vegetable-Pork Rolls (P.24)
4 珍珠包子：作法見第25頁　Pearl Rolls (P.25)
5 滑蝦包子：作法見第26頁　Shrimp Buns (P.26)

梅干肉包

材料：
外皮：與水煎包相同（見第18頁）
內餡：

絞肉	225公克
梅干菜	150公克
醬油	1大匙
糖	1小匙
鹽	$\frac{1}{2}$小匙
酒、胡椒粉、味精	各少許

❶梅干菜泡軟、洗淨、擠乾水分（圖1），再切細末（圖2）。

❷將內餡材料炒熟後，入蒸鍋大火蒸15分鐘，取出待涼，略為冷凍使其凝固（圖3）。

❸外皮揉勻後，分成25等份（圖4），每份包入1大匙內餡，放置醒40分鐘，再入蒸鍋大火蒸5分鐘即可。

Pork and Preserved Greens Buns

INGREDIENTS:
Dough: Same as for Steam Fried Pork Rolls (p. 18).

Filling:

225g (½ lb.)	ground pork
150g (⅓ lb.)	dried Chinese preserved mustard greens (mei kan ts'ai)
1 T.	soy sauce
1 t.	sugar
½ t.	salt
dash each:	rice wine, white pepper

❶ Soak the Chinese preserved mustard greens until soft. Wash thoroughly, then squeeze out the excess water (illus. 1). Mince finely (illus. 2).

❷ Stir-fry the filling ingredients untill cooked through, then place in a steamer and steam 15 minutes over high heat. Remove and allow to cool. Freeze until partially solid (illus. 3).

❸ Knead the dough until smooth, then divide into 25 equally sized portions (illus. 4). Wrap one tablespoon filling inside each piece of dough. Allow to rise for 40 minutes. Arrange in a steamer and steam for 5 minutes over high heat.

滷肉包子

材料：
外皮：與水煎包相同（見第18頁）
內餡：

五花肉帶皮	300公克
冬菜	37公克
醬油	2大匙
糖	1大匙
酒	1大匙
味精	少許
五香粉	少許
油	1大匙

❶ 五花肉絞碎備用。冬菜洗淨，先用1大匙油炒香，再放入絞肉及調味料炒熟，續入2杯水用小火燉燒至肉皮爛透（圖1），取出放涼再略爲冷凍使其凝固。

❷ 外皮揉勻後，分成20等份（圖2），每份包入一份內餡（圖3）捏成包子狀（圖4），再放置醒1小時使其酸透。

❸ 蒸鍋燒開，放入醒過之包子，大火蒸8分鐘即可。

Soy-Stewed Pork Buns

INGREDIENTS:
Dough: Same as for Steam Fried Pork Rolls (p. 18).

Filling:

300g (²⁄₃ lb.)	pork belly meat (half lean, half fat), with rind
37g (1½ oz.)	Chinese preserved cabbage (tung ts'ai)
2 T.	soy sauce
1 T.	sugar
1 T.	rice wine
dash	Chinese five-spice powder
1 T.	cooking oil

❶ Mince the pork belly meat (or have your butcher grind it for you). Rinse the Chinese preserved cabbage and stir-fry in one tablespoon cooking oil. Add the ground pork and the seasonings and continue to stir-fry until the meat is cooked through. Add 2 cups water and simmer over low heat until the pork rind is cooked soft (illus. 1). Remove from the wok or frying pan and freeze until partially solid.

❷ Knead the dough until smooth and divide into 20 equally sized portions (illus. 2). Wrap one portion of filling in each piece of dough (illus. 3) and pinch into the shape of a Chinese steamed bun (illus. 4). Allow to rise for one hour to achieve maximum bulk.

❸ Bring water to a boil in a steamer, and arrange the buns on the steaming racks. Steam 8 minutes over high heat and serve.

菜肉包子

材料：

外皮：與水煎包相同（見第18頁）

內餡：

絞腿肉	300公克
青江菜	300公克
水	4大匙
香油	1大匙
醬油	2小匙
鹽	1小匙
糖	1小匙
酒	1小匙
味精	$\frac{1}{2}$小匙
葱、薑、蒜	各少許
胡椒粉	少許

❶青江菜先燙熟，取出漂冷水（圖1），再剁細擠乾水份（圖2）。

❷青江菜和其它內餡材料拌勻（圖3）備用。

❸外皮揉勻後，分成30等份，每份包入1大匙內餡（圖4），再放置醒40分鐘，續入蒸鍋大火蒸6分鐘即可。

Vegetable-Pork Rolls

INGREDIENTS:

Dough: Same as for Steam Fried Pork Rolls (p.18).

Filling:

300g (²/₃ lb.)	ground pork
300g (²/₃ lb.)	*ch'ing kang ts'ai* (or Chinese cabbage)
4 T.	water
1 T.	sesame oil
2 t.	soy sauce
1 t.	salt
1 t.	sugar
1 t.	rice wine
as desired	minced green onion, minced ginger root, minced garlic
pinch	white pepper

❶ Blanch the leaves of the *ch'ing kang ts'ai* or Chinese cabbage briefly in boiling water. Remove and cool in tap water (illus. 1). Mince finely, then squeeze out excess moisture (illus. 2).

❷ Mix the minced greens with the other meat filling ingredients until well combined (illus. 3).

❸ Knead the dough until smooth and divide into 30 equally sized portions. Wrap one tablespoon filling inside each piece of dough (illus. 4). Allow the filled rolls to rise 40 minutes. Arrange in a steamer, and steam for 6 minutes over high heat.

珍珠包子

材料：
外皮：與水煎包相同（見第18頁）
內餡：

絞肉	75公克
糯米	1杯
油葱酥（圖1）	$\frac{1}{4}$杯
青豆	$\frac{1}{4}$杯
香菇末	$\frac{1}{4}$杯
水	$\frac{1}{4}$杯
香油	3大匙
醬油	1大匙
糖	$\frac{1}{2}$小匙
鹽	$\frac{1}{2}$小匙
味精	少許
胡椒粉	少許

❶糯米洗淨後，加1杯水蒸熟（約30分）（圖2）。
❷絞肉炒熟後，加入其它配料和調味料煮熟，續入糯米飯拌炒均勻（圖3）放涼。
❸外皮揉好後，分成30等份，每份包入1大匙內餡（圖4），放置醒40分鐘，續入蒸鍋大火蒸6分鐘即可。

Pearl Rolls

INGREDIENTS:
Dough: Same as for Steam Fried Pork Rolls (p. 18).

Filling:
75g (2⅔ oz.)	ground pork
1 c.	glutinous (mochi) rice
¼ c.	fried green onion flakes (illus. 1)
¼ c.	peas
¼ c.	dried Chinese black mushroom, soaked till soft and minced finely
¼ c.	water
3 T.	sesame oil
1 T.	soy sauce
½ t.	sugar
½ t.	salt
pinch	white pepper

❶ Wash the glutinous rice. Add one cup water to the rice and steam until cooked through, about 30 minutes (illus. 2).
❷ Fry the ground pork until cooked through, then add the other ingredients and seasonings and cook until done. Add the cooked glutinous rice and mix until well combined (illus. 3). Allow to cool.
❸ Knead the dough until smooth and divide into 30 equally sized portions. Wrap one tablespoon filling in each piece of dough (illus. 4). Allow to rise 40 minutes. Arrange in a steamer and steam 6 minutes over high heat.

滑蝦包子

Shrimp Buns

材料：
外皮：與水煎包相同（見第18頁）
內餡：

蝦仁	300公克
葱白末	2根
蛋白	1個
竹筍丁	$\frac{1}{2}$杯
絞肥肉	$\frac{1}{4}$杯
白醬油	2大匙
太白粉	2大匙
薑末	1匙
酒	1小匙
味精	$\frac{1}{2}$小匙
鹽	$\frac{1}{4}$小匙
胡椒粉	少許

❶蝦仁洗淨，吸乾水份（圖1），再剁成細丁狀（圖2）。
❷將內餡材料一起調味拌勻後略凍（圖3）。
❸外皮揉勻後，分成30等份，每份各包入1大匙內餡（圖4），再放置40分鐘，續入蒸鍋大火蒸5分鐘即可。

INGREDIENTS:
Dough: Same as for Steam Fried Pork Rolls, (p. 18).

Filling:

300g (²⁄₃ lb.)	fresh shrimp, shelled
2	green onions, minced (white part only)
1	egg white
½ c.	bamboo shoots, diced
¼ c.	ground fat pork
2 T.	light-colored soy sauce
2 T.	cornstarch
1 t.	minced ginger root
1 t.	rice wine
¼ t.	salt
pinch	white pepper

❶ Wash the shrimp and squeeze out the excess moisture (illus. 1). Dice finely (illus. 2).
❷ Mix the filling ingredients, including seasonings, until well combined. Freeze until partially solid (illus. 3).
❸ Knead the dough until smooth and divide into 30 equally sized portions. Wrap one tablespoon filling inside each piece of dough (illus. 4). Allow to rise 40 minutes. Arrange in a steamer and steam 5 minutes over high heat.

小籠包

Mini Steamed Pork Buns

材料：
外皮：發酵部份與水煎包相同（見第18頁）
　　燙麵：中筋麵粉 ⋯⋯⋯⋯225公克
　　　　　滾開水 ⋯⋯⋯⋯187公克
內餡：
　　絞上肉 ⋯⋯⋯⋯⋯⋯300公克
　　葱花 ⋯⋯⋯⋯⋯⋯⋯1杯
　　水 ⋯⋯⋯⋯⋯⋯⋯⋯½杯
　　香油 ⋯⋯⋯⋯⋯⋯⋯2大匙
　　薑末 ⋯⋯⋯⋯⋯⋯⋯1大匙
　　醬油 ⋯⋯⋯⋯⋯⋯⋯2小匙
　　糖 ⋯⋯⋯⋯⋯⋯⋯⋯1小匙
　　鹽 ⋯⋯⋯⋯⋯⋯⋯⋯½小匙
　　味精 ⋯⋯⋯⋯⋯⋯⋯½小匙
　　酒、胡椒粉 ⋯⋯⋯⋯⋯各少許

❶ 酸麵、燙麵分別揉勻後（圖1），放置醒30分鐘。

❷ 內餡所有材料拌勻後甩打數下（圖2），再略為冰凍。

❸ 醒過之酸麵、燙麵均勻地揉在一起，分成50等份（圖3），再包入2小匙內餡，入蒸鍋大火蒸4分鐘即可。

INGREDIENTS:
Yeast dough: Same as for Steam Fried Pork Rolls (p. 18).
Hot water dough:

| 225g (½ lb.) | all-purpose (medium gluten) flour |
| 187g (6½ oz.) | boiling water |

Filling:

300g (⅔ lb.)	ground pork
1 c.	chopped green onion
½ c.	water
2 T.	sesame oil
1 T.	minced ginger root
2 t.	soy sauce
1 t.	sugar
½ t.	salt
dash each:	rice wine, white pepper

❶ Mix and knead the yeast dough and hot water dough separately (illus. 1). Allow to rise for 30 minutes.

❷ Mix the filling ingredients until well blended. Fling against a counter or cutting board several times to increase the elasticity of the filling (illus. 2). Freeze until partially solid.

❸ Knead the yeast and hot water doughs together until well combined. Divide into 50 equally sized portions (illus. 3). Wrap two teaspoons filling in each portion of dough. Arrange in a steamer and steam over high heat for 4 minutes.

叉燒包

材料：
外皮：
《麵種》
低筋麵粉 ···················· 220公克
水 ························· 112公克
活酵母 ······················ 3.7公克

① {
低筋麵粉 ················· 187公克
糖 ······················· 112公克
蛋白 ························· 1個
油、白醋 ··············· 各1大匙
泡打粉（圖1）············· 1小匙
胺粉（圖1）·············· $\frac{1}{2}$小匙
}

❶麵種先揉勻後，醱酵3小時（圖2），續拌入①料揉拌成麵糰（圖3），再分成每份40克重之外皮。

❷每份麵皮包入2大匙內餡（內餡作法見附註），再入蒸鍋，大火蒸12分鐘即可。

■叉燒包內餡作法

叉燒肉 ······················ 200公克
叉燒醬：
水 ························· 150公克
糖 ·························· 50公克
醬油 ························· 2小匙
蠔油 ························· 2小匙
鹽 ·························· 1小匙
味精 ························· 1小匙
黃色5號 ····················· 少許
葱、薑、八角 ············· 各少許

② {
水 ························· 75公克
低筋麵粉 ·················· 37公克
沙拉油 ····················· 4小匙
玉米粉 ····················· 1小匙
太白粉 ····················· 1小匙
澄粉 ······················· 1小匙
}

❶叉燒肉切細丁。

❷叉燒醬煮開後，用②料芶芡、放涼，再拌入叉燒肉即爲內餡。

Roast Pork Buns

INGREDIENTS:
Dough Starter:

220g(7 3/4 oz.)	low gluter (cake) flour
112g(1/4 lb.)	water
1t.	active dry yeast

Dough:

①	187g (6½ oz.)	low gluten (cake) flour
	112g (¼ lb.)	sugar
	1	egg
	1 T. each	cooking oil, rice vinegar
	1 t.	baking powder (illus. 1)
	½ t.	ammonia bicarbonate (illus. 1)

❶ Mix the dough starter ingredients, knead until smooth, and allow to rise for 3 hours (illus. 2). Mix in ① and knead until smooth (illus.3). Divide into 40g (1⅓ oz.) portions.

❷ Wrap two tablespoons of filling (see recipe below) in each piece of dough. Arrange in a steamer. Steam over high heat for 12 minutes.

■ Procedure for making filling:

Filling:

200g (7 oz.)	Cantonese style roast pork (*cha siu*)

Sauce for filling:

150g (⅓ lb.)	water
50g (1¾ oz.)	sugar
2 t.	soy sauce
2 t.	oyster sauce
1 t.	salt
small amount each:	green onion, ginger root, star anise, red food coloring

②	75g (2⅔ oz.)	water
	37g (1⅓ oz.)	low gluten (cake) flour
	4 t.	cooking oil
	2 t.	cornstarch
	1 t.	wheat starch

❶ Dice the Cantonese style roast pork.

❷ Mix the sauce ingredients for the filling, and bring to a boil. Thicken with ② . Allow to cool, then stir in the diced roast pork.

①

②

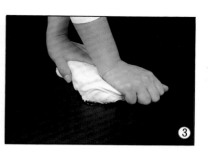
③

破酥甜包

Broken Flaky Sweet Rolls

材料：
外皮：

①
中筋麵粉 ……………300公克
水 …………………150公克
糖 …………………37公克
酵母 ………………11公克
泡打粉 ……………1小匙

②
中筋麵粉 ……………150公克
熱開水 ……………120公克

③
中筋麵粉 ……………225公克
熱油 ………………187公克

內餡：

熟白芝蔴粉 ……………225公克

細糖 ……………………150公克

熟猪油 …………………112公克

❶①、②、③分別揉勻成麵糰，①之麵糰再放置醒約40分鐘。
❷醒過之麵糰，與②之麵糰揉勻，再提成30×50公分的薄麵皮(圖1)。
❸將③之麵糰均勻地塗於提開之麵皮上(圖2)，再捲成長條狀(圖3)，而後分成50等份。
❹將內餡拌勻備用。
❺將每一份麵皮提薄，包入 1小匙內餡，放置醒30分鐘，再入蒸鍋大火蒸6分鐘即可。

INGREDIENTS:
Dough:

①
300g (2/3 lb.)   all-purpose (medium gluten) flour
150g (1/3 lb.)   water
37g (1 1/3 oz.)   sugar
11g (1/2 oz.)   active dry yeast
1 t.   baking powder

②
150g (1/3 lb.)   all-purpose flour
120g (1/4 lb.)   boiling water

③
225g (1/2 lb.)   all-purpose flour
187g (6 1/2 oz.)   hot cooking oil

Filling:

225g (1/2 lb.)   toasted white sesame seeds

150g (1/3 lb.)   sugar

112g (1/4 lb.)   lard (cooked)

❶ Mix separately the ingredients in ① , ② , and ③ to form three portions of dough. Allow dough ① to rise for about 40 minutes.
❷ After it has risen, knead dough ① together with dough ② . Roll out into a thin 30 x 50cm (12″ x 20″) rectangle (illus. 1).
❸ Spread dough ③ over the rolled dough rectangle (illus. 2), then roll it up into a long cylindrical shape (illus. 3). Divide into 50 equally sized portions.
❹ Mix the filling ingredients until well combined.
❺ Roll out thinly each portion of dough, and wrap one teaspoon filling in each. Allow to rise 30 minutes. Arrange in a steamer and steam over high heat for 6 minutes.

胡椒餅

Pepper Pork Rolls

材料：

外皮：

中筋麵粉	600公克
糖	37公克
泡打粉	1小匙
沙拉油	2大匙
酵母	26公克
水	$1\frac{1}{2}$杯
白芝蔴	1杯

內餡：

瘦肉	450公克
肥猪肉	150公克
葱花	1杯
香菜	$\frac{1}{2}$杯
蠔油	1大匙
糖	1大匙
醬油	1大匙
酒	1大匙
香油	1大匙
黑胡椒粉	1小匙
鹽	$\frac{1}{2}$小匙
味精	少許

❶瘦肉切粗粒、肥猪肉切細小丁，香菜切末，再把其它材料調味料均加入拌勻略凍。

❷酵母先溶於水後，再加入外皮之其它材料揉勻，放置醒40分鐘。

❸將醸過之外皮提成一張薄麵皮，擦上沙拉油（圖1）。捲成1長捲（圖2），再分成30等份。

❹每份麵皮壓扁，包入1大匙內餡，底部用水沾濕，再沾上芝蔴（圖3），續入180℃（360℉）烤箱，烤至底部金黃，有肉汁滲出即可。

INGREDIENTS:

Dough:

600g (1⅓ lb.)	all-purpose (medium gluten) flour
37g (1⅓ oz.)	sugar
1 t.	baking powder
2 T.	cooking oil
26g (1 oz.)	active dry yeast
1½ c.	water
1 c.	white sesame seed

Filling:

450g (1 lb.)	lean pork
150g (⅓ lb.)	fat pork
1 c.	chopped green onion
½ c.	fresh coriander (cilantro; Chinese parsley)
1 T.	sesame oil
1 T.	oyster sauce
1 T.	sugar
1 T.	soy sauce
1 T.	rice wine
1 t.	black pepper
½ t.	salt

❶ Dice the lean pork and the fat pork. Mince the fresh coriander and mix together with the other filling ingredients until well blended. Freeze until partially solid.

❷ Dissolve the yeast in the water. Mix into the other dough ingredients and knead until smooth. Allow to rise 40 minutes.

❸ After the rising is completed, roll the dough into a thin square. Spread some cooking oil over the surface of the dough (illus. 1) and roll into a long cylindrical shape (illus. 2). Divide the dough into 30 equally sized portions.

❹ Flatten each portion of dough, then wrap one tablespoon of filling inside. Dip the bottoms in water, then dip in the white sesame seeds (illus. 3). Arrange on a cookie sheet and bake in a 180°C (360°F) oven until the bottoms are golden brown and juice from the filling starts to seep out.

咖哩麵包

材料：

外皮：

中筋麵粉	300公克
糖	37公克
沙拉油	1大匙
泡打粉	1大匙
水	$\frac{3}{4}$杯
酵母	1大匙

內餡：

絞肉	150公克
洋葱絲	1杯
紅蘿蔔絲	$\frac{1}{2}$杯
葱花	$\frac{1}{2}$杯
木耳絲	$\frac{1}{2}$杯
蛋	2個
咖哩粉	1大匙
鹽	1小匙
糖	1小匙
胡椒粉、酒、香油、味精	各少許
①太白粉、水	各適量
沙拉油	3小匙
麵包粉	3杯

❶酵母先溶於水，再把外皮之其它材料拌勻揉成麵糰，再分成30等份。

❷蛋先用1小匙沙拉油炒成蛋花，起鍋(圖1)。鍋燒熱，入2小匙沙拉油將內餡之其他材料及調味料炒熟，以①料勾芡，再倒入蛋花拌勻備用。

❸每份麵皮包入將1大匙內餡，捏合(圖2)，入水中沾濕起出，再滾上麵包粉(圖3)。

❹炸油半鍋，熱至120℃(250℉)時，投入沾裹麵包粉之麵包，炸至金黃色撈起，瀝油即可。

Fried Curry Rolls

INGREDIENTS:

Dough:

300g (²⁄₃ lb.)	all-purpose (medium gluten) flour
37g (1¹⁄₃ oz.)	sugar
1 T.	cooking oil
1 T.	baking powder
¾ c.	water
1 T.	active dry yeast

Filling:

150g (¹⁄₃ lb.)	ground pork
1 c.	onion, julienned
½ c.	carrot, julienned
½ c.	chopped green onion
½ c.	wood ears, soaked until soft and julienned
2	eggs
1 T.	curry powder
1 t.	salt
1 t.	sugar
dash each:	white pepper, rice wine, sesame oil
as needed:	cornstarch, water
3 t.	cooking oil
3 c.	fine bread crumbs

❶ Dissolve the yeast in the water, then mix together with the other dough ingredients until smooth. Divide into 30 equally sized portions.

❷ Beat the eggs lightly, then scramble in one teaspoon oil. Remove from wok (illus. 1). Heat the wok, add two teaspoons cooking oil, then stir-fry the filling ingredients with the seasonings until cooked through. Thicken with ① , then mix in the scrambled egg.

❸ Wrap one tablespoon of filling in each piece of dough, then pinch to seal (illus. 2). Dip in water to moisten and roll in fine bread crumbs (illus. 3).

❹ Fill a wok or deep-fryer half-full with cooking oil and heat to 120°C (250°F). Deep-fry the curry rolls until golden brown. Remove from the oil and drain.

①

②

③

蟹黃小包

材料：
外皮：與水煎包相同（見第18頁）
內餡：
　　鮮肉餡與小籠包同（見第27頁），但份量減半
　　　┌ 蟹肉⋯⋯⋯⋯⋯⋯⋯⋯75公克
　　　│ 洋葱末⋯⋯⋯⋯⋯⋯⋯½杯
　　　│ 太白粉水⋯⋯⋯⋯⋯⋯2大匙
　　　│ 醬油⋯⋯⋯⋯⋯⋯⋯⋯1小匙
①　│ 糖⋯⋯⋯⋯⋯⋯⋯⋯⋯1小匙
　　　│ 咖哩粉⋯⋯⋯⋯⋯⋯⋯1小匙
　　　│ 鹽⋯⋯⋯⋯⋯⋯⋯⋯⋯½小匙
　　　│ 味精、酒、胡椒粉⋯⋯⋯⋯⋯
　　　└ ⋯⋯⋯⋯⋯⋯⋯⋯⋯各少許
油 ⋯⋯⋯⋯⋯⋯⋯⋯⋯⋯⋯2小匙

❶鮮肉餡先拌勻，①料另外以2小匙油炒勻待涼，再
　分別略爲冷凍，使其凝固。
❷外皮分成30份，每份先包入1小匙鮮肉餡，再放入
　1小匙蟹肉（圖1），而後捏成包子狀（圖2），上留
　一小洞（圖3）放置醒40分鐘，再入蒸鍋大火蒸5分
　鐘即可。

Golden Crab Rolls

INGREDIENTS:
Dough: Same as for Steam Fried Pork Rolls (p. 18).

Filling:
half recipe	filling for Mini Steamed Pork Buns (p. 27)
75g (2¾ oz.)	fresh crab meat
½ c.	minced onion
2 T.	cornstarch dissolved in water
1 t.	soy sauce
1 t.	sugar
1 t.	curry powder
½ t.	salt
dash each:	rice wine, white pepper
2 t.	cooking oil

(① groups the rows from 75g through dash each)

❶ First mix the meat filling until well combined. Heat a wok, add two teaspoons oil, then stir-fry ① until cooked through. Allow to cool, then freeze until partially solid.

❷ Divide the dough into 30 equally sized portions. Place one teaspoon of filling inside a piece of dough, then add one teaspoon crab meat filling (illus. 1). Pinch the dough over the filling (illus. 2), leaving only a small opening at the top (illus. 3). Repeat for each piece of dough. Allow to rise 40 minutes. Arrange in a steamer and steam for 5 minutes.

地瓜芝蔴包

材料：
外皮：與豆沙小包相同(見第14頁)
內餡：
　　去皮地瓜 ⋯⋯⋯⋯⋯⋯300公克　　糖⋯⋯⋯⋯⋯⋯⋯⋯⋯⋯75公克
　　熟黑芝蔴粉(圖4)⋯⋯⋯75公克　　熟猪油⋯⋯⋯⋯⋯⋯⋯⋯75公克

❶地瓜蒸熟後，搗碎(圖5)，再加入其他材料拌匀成內餡(圖6)。
❷每份外皮，包入1大匙內餡，放置醒40分鐘，再入蒸鍋大火蒸5分鐘
　即可。

Sesame-Yam Rolls

INGREDIENTS:
Dough: Same as for Red Bean Paste Buns (p. 14).

Filling:
300g (²/₃ lb.)	yams or sweet potatoes, pared
75g (2²/₃ oz.)	black sesame seed, toasted and ground into a powder (illus.4)
75g (2²/₃ oz.)	sugar
75g (2²/₃ oz.)	lard (cooked)

❶ Steam the yams or sweet potatoes until soft and mash unt
smooth (illus. 5). Mix in the other filling ingredients until we
blended to form the filling (illus. 6).
❷ Wrap one tablespoon of filling inside each portion of dough. A
low to rise 40 minutes. Arrange in a steamer and steam over hig
heat for 5 minutes.

1 三鮮蒸餃：作法見第40頁
2 淨素蒸餃：作法見第41頁
3 鮮肉蒸餃：作法見第42頁
4 四喜蒸餃：作法見第43頁

1 Pork-Seafood Steamed Dumplings (P.40)
2 Vegetarian Steamed Dumplings (P.41)
3 Steamed Pork Dumplings (P.42)
4 Four Color Steamed Dumplings (P.43)

三鮮蒸餃

Pork-Seafood Steamed Dumplings

材料：
外皮：
　中筋麵粉 ……300公克
　熱開水 ……………1杯

內餡：
　絞腿肉 ………150公克
　蝦仁 …………112公克
　干貝(蒸軟)……37公克
　葱花………………¼杯
　香油 ……………2大匙
　薑末 ……………1大匙
　醬油 ……………1大匙
　鹽………………½小匙
　胡椒粉、酒……各少許

沾料：
　熱開水 …………2大匙
　薑末 ……………1大匙
　白醋 ……………1大匙
　鹽、味精、香油各少許
　調勻

❶蝦仁洗淨，吸乾水份，略爲剁碎(圖1)，干貝撕成細絲(圖2)。
❷將內餡材料一起拌勻，略爲冷凍。
❸將外皮材料揉勻，分成如一節拇指大小之麵糰(圖3)，提薄後包入2小匙內餡(圖4)，入蒸鍋大火蒸5分鐘即可。
❹食時沾沾料。

INGREDIENTS:
Dough:
300g (⅔ lb.)	all-purpose (medium gluten) flour
1 c.	boiling water

Filling:
150g (⅓ lb.)	ground pork (leg meat)
112g (¼ lb.)	shrimp, shelled
37g (1⅓ oz.)	dried scallops, steamed soft
¼ c.	chopped green onion
2 T.	sesame oil
1 T.	minced ginger root
1 T.	soy sauce
½ t.	salt
dash each:	white pepper, rice wine

Dipping sauce:
2 T.	water
1 T.	minced ginger root
1 T.	rice vinegar
dash each:	salt, sesame oil

❶ Wash the shrimp and squeeze out the excess moisture. Chop coarsely (illus. 1). Tear the steamed dried scallops into fine shreds (illus. 2).
❷ Mix the filling ingredients together until well combined and freeze until partially solid.
❸ Knead the dough ingredients until smooth. Break into pieces about the size of a thumb joint (illus. 3). Roll thin and wrap two teaspoons filling inside each (illus. 4). Arrange in a steamer and steam over high heat for 5 minutes.
❹ Dip in the dipping sauce before eating.

淨素蒸餃

材料：
外皮：與三鮮蒸餃相同（見第40頁）
內餡：

　　青江菜 …………………300公克
　　煮熟鮮竹筍 ……………300公克
　　香菇…………………………37公克
　　硬白豆干 …………………1塊
① ┌ 香油 …………………5大匙
　├ 味精……………………½小匙
　├ 鹽…………………………½小匙
　└ 胡椒粉…………………少許

❶青江菜先燙熟、漂涼、再切碎，擠乾水份。
❷香菇、竹筍、硬白豆干分別切碎，加①料炒香放涼
　，再拌入青江菜（圖1）。
❸外皮分成35等份，每份揑薄（圖2），各包入1大匙
　內餡，揑成半月形（圖3），入蒸籠大火蒸5分鐘即
　可。
■沾料可用薑米醋（圖4）。

Vegetarian Steamed Dumplings

INGREDIENTS:
Dough: Same as for Pork-Seafood Steamed
　　　　Dumplings (p. 40).

Filling:
300g (⅔ lb.)	*ch'ing kang ts'ai* or other leafy stalk green
300g (⅔ lb.)	cooked fresh bamboo shoots
37g (1⅓ oz.)	dried Chinese black mushrooms
1 cake	firm white pressed bean curd
① ⎰ 5 T. ⎱ ½ t. pinch	sesame oil salt white pepper

❶ Parboil the *ch'ing kang ts'ai* or other greens until cooked through, then cool in tap water. Mince finely, then squeeze out the excess moisture.

❷ Soak the dried mushrooms until soft. Mince the mushrooms, bamboo shoots, and pressed bean curd separately. Stir-fry together with ① , allow to cool, then add the minced greens (illus. 1).

❸ Divide the dough into 35 equal portions, then roll each portion into a thin circle (illus. 2). Wrap one tablespoon filling in each circle of dough and pinch into a cresent shape (illus. 3). Arrange in a steamer and steam over high heat for 5 minutes.

■ May be dipped in ginger vinegar before eating (illus. 4).

鮮肉蒸餃

材料：
外皮：與三鮮蒸餃相同（見第40頁）
內餡：

絞上肉 ……………………300公克	
香菇 ……………………6朵	
葱花…………………………$\frac{1}{4}$杯	
薑末 ……………………1大匙	

① 水 ………………………3大匙
香油 ……………………2大匙
醬油 ……………………1大匙
太白粉 …………………1大匙
鹽………………………$\frac{1}{2}$小匙
糖………………………$\frac{1}{2}$小匙
味精…………………………$\frac{1}{4}$小匙
胡椒粉、酒、鮮味露…各少許

❶香菇泡軟切末（圖1），和其它材料、①料拌勻略冷凍。
❷外皮分成35等份（圖2），每份提薄（圖3），各包入1大匙內餡後（圖4），入蒸籠大火蒸6分鐘即可。
❸食時可沾薑米醋。

Steamed Pork Dumplings

INGREDIENTS:
Dough: Same as for Pork-Seafood Steamed Dumplings (p. 40).

Filling:

300g ($\frac{2}{3}$ lb.)	ground pork
6	dried Chinese black mushrooms
$\frac{1}{4}$ c.	chopped green onion
1 T.	minced ginger root

① 3 T. — water
2 T. — sesame oil
1 T. — soy sauce
1 T. — cornstarch
$\frac{1}{2}$ t. — sugar
$\frac{1}{2}$ t. — salt
dash each: — white pepper, rice wine, Maggi sauce

❶ Soak the mushrooms until soft and mince (illus. 1). Mix with the rest of the filling ingredients and ① . Freeze until partially solid.
❷ Divide the dough into 35 equally sized portions (illus. 2). Roll each piece of dough thin (illus. 3), and wrap one tablespoon of filling in each (illus. 4). Arrange in steamer and steam over high heat for 6 minutes.
❸ The dumplings can be dipped in ginger vinegar before eating.

四喜蒸餃

材料：
外皮：與三鮮蒸餃相同（見第40頁），份量減半。
內餡：

絞腿肉	225公克
蝦仁	112公克
薑末	1大匙
紅蘿蔔末	3大匙
香菇末	3大匙
火腿末	3大匙
靑江菜末	3大匙

①
- 醬油 …… 1大匙
- 香油 …… 1大匙
- 太白粉 …… 1大匙
- 鹽 …… $\frac{1}{2}$小匙
- 味精 …… $\frac{1}{4}$小匙
- 胡椒粉、酒、鮮味露… 各少許

❶外皮分成20等份。
❷蝦仁剁碎後，加絞肉、薑末及①料拌勻略凍（圖1）
❸每份麵皮提開後，包入1大匙內餡（圖2），捏成4孔餃子（圖3），在每一孔內塞入一種蔬菜末（圖4），入蒸籠大火蒸6分鐘即可。

Four Color Steamed Dumplings

INGREDIENTS:
Dough: Half a recipe of the dough used to make Pork-Seafood Steamed Dumplings (p. 40).

Filling:

225g (½ lb.)	ground pork (leg meat)
112g (¼ lb.)	shrimp, shelled
1 T.	minced ginger root
3 T.	minced carrot
3 T.	dried Chinese black mushrooms, soaked until soft and minced
3 T.	minced ham
3 T.	minced *ch'ing kang ts'ai* or other leafy green

①
- 1 T. — sesame oil
- 1 T. — cornstarch
- 1 T. — soy sauce
- ½ t. — salt
- dash each: white pepper, rice wine, Maggi sauce

❶ Divide the dough into 20 equally sized portions.
❷ Chop the shrimp coarsely, then mix in the ground pork, minced ginger root, and ① until well combined. Freeze until partially solid (illus. 1).
❸ Roll out each piece of dough until thin. Wrap one tablespoon of filling in each (illus. 2), then pinch at the top to form four pockets (illus. 3). For each dumpling, place a small amount of each of the last four (minced) ingredients in each pocket, so that the dumpling has four colors on its top (illus. 4). Arrange in a steamer and steam over high heat for 6 minutes.

1 珍珠燒賣：作法見第46頁
2 蟹黃燒賣：作法見第47頁
1 Pearl Siu Mai (P.46)
2 Crab Siu Mai (P.47)

珍珠燒賣

材料：

外皮：與三鮮蒸餃同（見第40頁）

內餡：

糯米、水‥‥‥‥‥‥‥‥各 1 杯

① {
絞瘦肉‥‥‥‥‥‥‥‥75公克
蝦米‥‥‥‥‥‥‥‥‥37公克
香菇（切絲）‥‥‥‥‥‥6朵
葱酥‥‥‥‥‥‥‥‥‥$\frac{1}{4}$ 杯
}

② {
香油‥‥‥‥‥‥‥‥‥2大匙
醬油‥‥‥‥‥‥‥‥‥1大匙
糖‥‥‥‥‥‥‥‥‥‥$\frac{1}{2}$ 小匙
鹽‥‥‥‥‥‥‥‥‥‥$\frac{1}{4}$ 小匙
味精‥‥‥‥‥‥‥‥‥少許
胡椒粉、酒‥‥‥‥‥各少許
}

青豆仁‥‥‥‥‥‥‥‥‥30粒

沙拉油‥‥‥‥‥‥‥‥‥4大匙

❶糯米洗淨，加 1 杯水煮熟。

❷油 4 大匙，炒香①料，續入②料炒熟，趁熱加入糯米飯拌勻（圖 1 ）。

❸外皮分成30等份（圖2），每份包入 1 大匙糯米餡（圖3），捏成石榴花狀，上面點綴一粒青豆仁（圖 4 ），入蒸鍋大火蒸 6 分鐘即可。

Pearl Siu Mai

INGREDIENTS:

Dough: Same as for Pork-Seafood Steamed Dumplings (p. 40).

Filling:

1 c. each:		glutinous (mochi) rice, water
①	75g (2½ oz.)	lean ground pork
	37g (1⅓ oz.)	dried shrimp
	6	dried Chinese black mushrooms, soaked until soft and shredded
	¼ c.	fried green onion flakes
	30	green peas
	4 T.	cooking oil
②	2 T.	sesame oil
	1 T.	soy sauce
	½ t.	sugar
	¼ t.	salt
	dash each:	white pepper, rice wine

❶ Wash the glutinous rice. Add one cup water and cook until done.

❷ Fry ① in 4 tablespoons oil until fragrant. Add ② and stir-fry until cooked through. Stir in the cooked glutinous rice while still hot (illus. 1).

❸ Divide the dough into 30 equally sized portions. Wrap one tablespoon of the glutinous rice filling in each (illus. 2) and pinch into a frilled flower shape at the top (illus. 3). Garnish each with a pea (illus. 4). Arrange in a steamer and steam over high heat for 6 minutes.

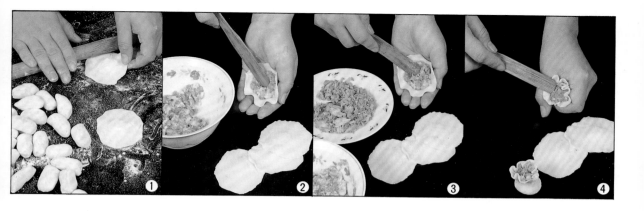

蟹黃燒賣

材料：
外皮：與三鮮蒸餃相同（見第40頁）
內餡：

①
絞上肉	……………	300公克
葱花	……………	$\frac{1}{2}$ 杯
醬油	……………	2大匙
香油	……………	2大匙
薑末	……………	1大匙
鹽	……………	$\frac{1}{2}$ 小匙
糖	……………	$\frac{1}{2}$ 小匙
味精	……………	$\frac{1}{4}$ 小匙
胡椒粉、酒	……………	各少許

②
蟹肉	……………	112公克
洋葱末	……………	$\frac{1}{4}$ 杯
葱花	……………	2大匙
太白粉、水	……………	各2大匙
咖哩粉	……………	1小匙
蠔油	……………	1小匙
糖	……………	$\frac{1}{2}$ 小匙
味精	……………	$\frac{1}{8}$ 小匙
胡椒粉、酒	……………	各少許
香油	……………	少許
沙拉油	……………	1小匙

❶①料調味打勻，略冷凍。
❷②料用1小匙沙拉油炒熟放涼。
❸外皮分成40等份，每份提成外薄內厚之圓形（圖1）
，中間先壓入1小匙絞肉餡（圖2），再加$\frac{1}{2}$小匙蟹
肉（圖3），捏成石榴花形（圖4），入蒸籠大火蒸6
分鐘即可。

Crab Siu Mai

INGREDIENTS:
Dough: Same as for Pork-Seafood Steamed
          Dumplings (p. 40).

Filling:

①
300g ($\frac{2}{3}$ lb.)	ground pork
$\frac{1}{2}$ c.	chopped green onion
2 T.	soy sauce
2 T.	sesame oil
1 T.	minced ginger root
$\frac{1}{2}$ t.	salt
$\frac{1}{2}$ t.	sugar
pinch each:	white pepper, rice wine

②
112g ($\frac{1}{4}$ lb.)	crab meat
$\frac{1}{4}$ c.	minced onion
2 T.	chopped green onion
2 T. each:	cornstarch, water
1 t.	curry powder
1 t.	oyster sauce
$\frac{1}{2}$ t.	sugar
pinch each:	white pepper, rice wine
dash	sesame oil

1 t.   cooking oil

❶ Mix ① until well combined. Freeze until partially solid.
❷ Stir-fry ② in one teaspoon cooking oil until cooked through, then allow to cool.
❸ Divide the dough into 40 equally sized portions. Roll each portion into a circle with a thicker center and thinner outer edge (illus. 1). Press one teaspoon ground pork filling in the center of each circle of dough (illus. 2), then add $\frac{1}{2}$ teaspoon crab filling on top of the pork filling (illus. 3). Pinch into a frilled flower shape at the top (illus. 4). Arrange in a steamer and steam over high heat for 6 minutes.

翡翠魚餃

材料：
外皮：
中筋麵粉 ……300公克
菠菜 ……100公克
水……………… $\frac{1}{2}$ 杯
內餡：
鮪魚肉 ………150公克
肥豬油………75公克
青豆仁………37公克
紅蘿蔔末………37公克

① 白醬油 ………2大匙
香油 ………2大匙
鹽…………… $\frac{1}{2}$ 小匙
胡椒粉、酒、味精…
………………各少許

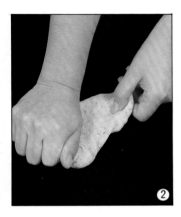

❶菠菜洗淨，加水用果汁機打碎後（圖1），倒入麵粉中揉勻成麵糰（圖2），分成40等份。
❷魚肉切細，肥肉剁碎後，加入其它材料及①料拌勻
❸每份外皮提薄後（圖3），包入1大匙內餡（圖4），入蒸鍋大火蒸6分鐘即可。

Emerald Fish Dumplings

INGREDIENTS:
Dough:
300g (²⁄₃ lb.)	all-purpose (medium gluten) flour
100g (3½ oz.)	fresh spinach
½ c.	water

Filling:
150g (⅓ lb.)	fresh tuna fillet
75g (2²⁄₃ oz.)	fat pork
37g (1⅓ oz.)	green peas
37g (1⅓ oz.)	minced carrot
① 2 T.	light-colored soy sauce
2 T.	sesame oil
½ t.	salt
dash each:	white pepper, rice wine

❶ Wash the spinach thoroughly, add the water, and puree in a blender (illus. 1). Pour into the flour and knead into a smooth dough (illus. 2). Divide the dough into 40 equally sized portions.
❷ Mince the tuna fillet and the fat pork. Add the other ingredients and ① and mix until well blended.
❸ Roll out each piece of dough until thin and flat (illus. 3). Wrap one tablespoon filling in each (illus. 4). Arrange in a steamer and steam over high heat for 6 minutes.

水晶蒸餃

Crystal Steamed Dumplings

材料：

外皮：

澄粉	112公克
元宵粉	112公克
太白粉	75公克
熱開水	1¼杯
沙拉油	1大匙

內餡：

絞肉	225公克
荸薺	8個
大蒜	6粒
油	3大匙

① | 水 | ⅓杯 |
蠔油	1小匙
糖	½小匙
鹽	¼小匙
味精	少許
胡椒粉、酒	各少許

② | 水 | 3大匙 |
| 麵粉 | 1大匙 |
| 澄粉 | 1大匙 |

❶荸薺剁碎後，擠去水份（圖1），大蒜也剁碎備用。

❷油3大匙炒香蒜末，續入絞肉炒熟，再入荸薺及①料炒熟，最後用②料勾芡放涼（圖2）。

❸外皮揉勻後，分成30等份，每份包入1小匙內餡（圖3），入蒸籠大火蒸6分鐘即可。

INGREDIENTS:

Dough:

112g (¼ lb.)	wheat starch
112g (¼ lb.)	glutinous rice flour
75g (2½ oz.)	cornstarch
1 T.	cooking oil
1¼ c.	boiling water

Filling:

225g (½ lb.)	ground pork
8	water chestnuts
6 cloves	garlic
3 T.	cooking

① | ⅓ c. | water |
1 t.	oyster sauce
½ t.	sugar
¼ t.	salt
dash each:	white pepper, rice wine

② | 3 T. | water |
| 1 T. each: | flour，wheat starch |

❶ Mince the water chestnuts and squeeze out the excess moisture (illus. 1). Mince the garlic.

❷ Heat 3 tablespoons oil in a wok and fry the minced garlic until fragrant. Add the ground pork and stir-fry until done. Add the minced water chestnuts and ① and stir-fry until cooked through. Thicken with ②. Remove from heat and allow to cool (illus. 2).

❸ Knead the dough ingredients until smooth. Divide the dough into 30 equally sized portions. Wrap 1 teaspoon filling in each (illus. 3). Arrange in a steamer and steam over high heat for 6 minutes.

烙薄餅

Mooshu Pancakes

材料：

中筋麵粉	300公克
熱開水	1杯
沙拉油	$\frac{1}{2}$杯

❶麵粉用熱開水揉拌成燙麵後，分成20等份。

❷每份麵皮壓扁後，在表面塗上沙拉油（圖1）。

❸將兩份麵皮對面壓合在一起（圖2），再用提麵棍提成直徑約12公分的薄餅。

❹平底鍋燒熱，再把薄餅放入，用小火乾烙至兩面變白色並膨起後，取出一分爲二即可（圖3）。

❺食時可包肉絲、牛肉、烤鴨等。

INGREDIENTS:

300g (⅔ lb.)	all-purpose (medium gluten) flour
1 c.	boiling water
½ c.	cooking oil

❶ Add the boiling water to the flour and knead into a smooth dough. Divide into 20 equally sized portions.

❷ Flatten each portion of dough, then brush some cooking oil over the top of each (illus. 1).

❸ Press the oiled dough pancakes together in pairs (illus. 2), then roll each into a 12cm (5″) pancake.

❹ Heat a dry flat-bottomed frying pan or griddle. Bake each of the pancakes slowly over low heat until both sides have turned white and begin to puff up. Remove from the heat and pull each pancake apart into two (illus. 3).

❺ Mooshu pancakes can be used to wrap stir-fried pork shreds, beef shreds, or Peking duck.

三鮮鍋貼

材料：

外皮：與三鮮蒸餃相同（見第40頁）

內餡：

絞上肉	……150公克	香油	……1½大匙
鷄胸肉	……150公克	醬油	……1大匙
蝦仁	……150公克	鹽	……1小匙
芹菜末	……½杯	糖	……½小匙
鷄湯	……3大匙	味精、胡椒粉、酒……	
薑末	……1大匙		……各少許
沙拉油	……4大匙		

❶鷄胸肉、蝦仁剁碎後，再把其它材料拌勻。

❷外皮分成40等份，每份提薄（圖1），包入內餡。

❸平底鍋入沙拉油4大匙燒熱，鍋貼排入（圖2），先用小火煎2分鐘，再加入一杯水，蓋上鍋蓋，用中火煎至水乾，底部呈金黃色，翻面（圖3），再煎兩分鐘即可。

Combo Pot Stickers

INGREDIENTS:

Dough: Same as for Pork-Seafood Steamed Dumplings (p. 40).

Filling:

150g (⅓ lb.)	ground pork
150g (⅓ lb.)	chicken breast fillet
150g (⅓ lb.)	shrimp, shelled
½ c.	minced Chinese celery
3 T.	chicken stock
1½ T.	sesame oil
1 T.	minced ginger root
1 T.	soy sauce
1 t.	salt
½ t.	sugar
pinch each:	white pepper, rice wine
4 T.	cooking oil

❶ Mince the chicken breast fillet and shelled shrimp finely, then add the other ingredients.

❷ Divide the dough into 40 equally sized portions. Roll each into a thin circle (illus. 1). Wrap some filling in each.

❸ Heat 4 tablespoons cooking oil in a flat-bottomed frying pan, then arrange the pot stickers in the pan (illus. 2). Fry over low heat for 2 minutes, then add 1 cup water and cover. Cook over medium heat until the water has evaporated and the pot stickers are golden brown. Turn over (illus. 3) and fry another 2 minutes.

②

①

③

牛舌餅

材料：

外皮：

《水油皮》

中筋麵粉 ⋯⋯300公克
熱開水 ⋯⋯⋯150公克
沙拉油 ⋯⋯⋯75公克

《油酥》

中筋麵粉 ⋯⋯225公克
沙拉油 ⋯⋯⋯112公克

內餡：

熟麵粉 ⋯⋯⋯⋯⋯1杯
蜂蜜 ⋯⋯⋯⋯⋯$\frac{3}{4}$杯
奶粉 ⋯⋯⋯⋯⋯$\frac{1}{2}$杯
糖粉 ⋯⋯⋯⋯⋯$\frac{1}{3}$杯
沙拉油 ⋯⋯⋯⋯$\frac{1}{4}$杯

❶ 外皮做法與元寶酥相同（見第58頁），分成25等份。
❷ 熟麵粉待涼後，再和其它內餡材料拌勻（圖1）。
❸ 每份外皮包入1大匙內餡，捏成長橢圓形（圖2），
　用平底鍋以中火煎至兩面金黃（圖3）即可。

Chinese Longjohns

INGREDIENTS:

Water-shortening dough:

300g (²⁄₃ lb.)	all-purpose (medium gluten) flour
150g (¹⁄₃ lb.)	boiling water
75g (2²⁄₃ oz.)	cooking oil

Flaky dough:

| 225g (½ lb.) | all-purpose (medium gluten) flour |
| 112g (¼ lb.) | cooking oil |

Filling:

1 c.	roasted flour
¾ c.	honey
½ c.	milk powder
⅓ c.	sugar
¼ c.	cooking oil

❶ Prepare the dough according to the method described in Silver Ingot Pastries (p. 58). Divide the dough into 25 equally sized portions.
❷ Mix the filling ingredients until well combined (illus. 1). Freeze until partially solid.
❸ Wrap one tablespoon filling in each piece of dough. Roll out into an oblong shape as shown (illus. 2). Bake each one on both sides over medium heat in a dry frying pan or griddle until golden (illus. 3).

1 元寶酥餅：作法見第58頁　Silver Ingot Pastries (P.58)
2 蓮蓉酥餅：作法見第58頁　Lotus Seed Pastries (P.58)
3 奶黃酥餅：作法見第59頁　Butter Cream Pastries (P.59)
4 蛋 黃 酥：作法見第60頁　Egg Yolk-Red Bean Pastries (P.60)
5 豬肉酥餅：作法見第61頁　Pork Pastries (P.61)

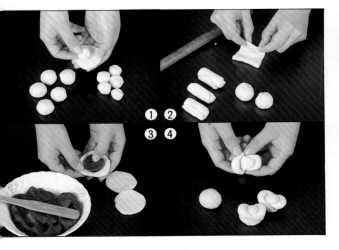
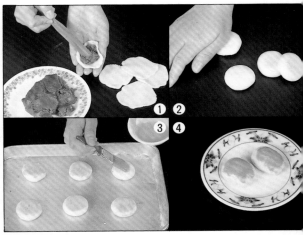

元寶酥餅

材料：

外皮：《水油皮》　　　　　《油酥》
　　中筋麵粉 ……300公克　　中筋麵粉 ……225公克
　　水 …………150公克　　猪油 …………112公克
　　猪油…………75公克　　內餡：
蛋黃 ……………1個　　黑豆沙 ………450公克

❶水油皮、油酥分別揉成麵糰後，各分成25等份，每
　份油酥包於水油皮內（圖1），即爲外皮麵糰。
❷將每個麵糰用麵棍提薄，折3折（圖2），作2次後
　，再略提薄，包入1大匙豆沙（圖3），做成元寶形
　（圖4）後，排入烤盤，上塗蛋黃,入200°C（390°F）
　烤箱烤至金黃色即可。

Silver Ingot Pastries

INGREDIENTS:
Water-shortening dough:
300g (²/₃ lb.)	all-purpose (medium gluten) flour
150g (¹/₃ lb.)	water
75g (3²/₃ oz.)	lard or shortening

Flaky dough:
225g (¹/₂ lb.)	all-purpose (medium gluten) flour
112g (¹/₄ lb.)	lard or shortening

Filling:
450g (1 lb.)	sweet red bean paste
1	egg yolk

❶ Mix and knead the two doughs separately. Divide
  each into 25 equally sized portions. Wrap one portion of flaky dough inside each piece of water-
  shortening dough (iilus. 1).
❷ Roll out each piece of dough until thin and fold into
  thirds (illus. 2). Repeat this process two more times.
  Roll out thin. Wrap one tablespoon bean paste in
  each (illus. 3) and form into the shape of an ingot,
  as illustrated (illus. 4). Arrange on a cookie sheet.
  Brush some egg yolk on the tops and bake at 200°C
  (390°C) until golden.

蓮蓉酥餅

材料：

外皮：與元寶酥相同（見第58頁）
內餡：蓮蓉……… 300公克
蛋黃 ………………1個

❶每份外皮包入2小匙蓮蓉餡（圖1），略壓扁（圖2）
　後，排入烤盤，上塗蛋黃（圖3），入200°C（390°F）
　烤箱烤至金黃色（圖4）即可。

Lotus Seed Pastries

INGREDIENTS:
Dough: Same as for Silver Ingot Pastries
　　　　(p. 58).

Filling:
300g (²/₃ lb.)	sweet lotus seed paste
1	egg yolk

❶ Wrap two teaspoons of filling in each
  piece of dough (illus. 1). Lightly press flat
  (illus. 2) and arrange on a cookie sheet.
  Brush some lightly beaten egg yolk on
  each (illus. 3). Bake at 200°C (390°F) until
  golden (illus. 4).

奶黃酥餅

材料：
外皮：與元寶酥相同（見第58頁）
內餡：

水	1杯
奶水	$\frac{1}{2}$杯
糖	$\frac{1}{2}$杯
軟凍粉	4大匙
麵粉	4大匙
玉米粉	2大匙
奶油	1大匙
香草片	4片
蛋黃	1個
黑、白芝蔴	少許

❶內餡材料調勻後，用小火煮熟，煮時需不斷地攪動（圖1），以免燒焦，煮熟後放涼，略爲冷凍。
❷外皮分成25等份，每份包入1大匙內餡（圖2），完成後略爲壓扁（圖3），即爲酥餅。
❸酥餅上塗蛋黃，並用黑、白芝蔴裝飾（圖4），續入200℃（390℉）烤箱烤至金黃色即可。

Butter Cream Pastries

INGREDIENTS:
Dough: Same as for Silver Ingot Pastries
(p. 58).

Filling:

1 c.	water
½ c.	sugar
½ c.	evaporated milk
4 T.	custard powder
4 T.	flour
2 T.	cornstarch
1 T.	butter
2 t.	vanilla extract
1	egg yolk
as needed	black, white sesame seeds

❶ Mix the filling ingredients together until blended. Cook over low heat, stirring constantly (illus. 1) to avoid scorching. After the filling is cooked through, allow to cool, then freeze until partially solid.
❷ Divide the dough into 25 equally sized portions. Wrap one tablespoon of filling in each piece of dough (illus. 2) and flatten each pastry lightly (illus. 3).
❸ Brush some lightly beaten egg yolk over the top of each pastry and sprinkle on some sesame seeds to garnish (illus. 4). Bake in a 200°C (390°F) oven until golden.

蛋黃酥

Egg Yolk-Red Bean Pastries

材料
外皮：
　《水油皮》
　　高筋麵粉……………… 150公克
　　水………………………… 75公克
　　豬油…………………………… 37公克
　《油酥》
　　低筋麵粉……………… 112公克
　　豬油……………………………… 56公克
內餡：
　　鹹蛋黃……………………… 6個
　　豆沙…………………………150公克
蛋黃……………………………………1個
黑芝蔴…………………………………少許

❶外皮分別揉勻後，各分成12等份，每份水油皮包油
　酥（圖1），擀開，折3折（圖2），再擀開，再折3
　折，備用。
❷鹹蛋黃先入烤箱烤熟（約8分鐘），再一分爲二。
❸豆沙分成12等份，每份包半個鹹蛋黃（圖3）。
❹麵皮再擀開，包入豆沙蛋黃餡，排於烤盤上，上塗
　蛋黃，再飾以芝蔴（圖4），入180℃（360°F）烤箱
　烤至金黃色即可（約20分鐘）。

INGREDIENTS:
Water-shortening dough:

150g (⅓ lb.)	high gluten (bread) flour
75g (2⅔ oz.)	water
37g (1⅓ oz.)	lard or shortening

Flaky dough:

112g (¼ lb.)	low gluten (cake) flour
56g (2 oz.)	lard or shortening

Filling:

6	yolks of salt-preserved eggs
150g (⅓ lb.)	sweet red bean paste
1	egg yolk
as needed	black sesame seeds

❶ Mix the ingredients for the water-shortening dough and the flaky dough separately until smooth. Divide each into 12 equally sized portions. Wrap one portion of flaky dough inside each portion of water-shortening dough (illus. 1). Roll out each piece of dough, then fold into thirds to form three layers. (illus. 2). Roll out again, and once more fold into thirds to form three layers.

❷ Bake the salt-preserved egg yolks in an oven until cooked through, about 8 minutes. Divide each egg yolk into two halves.

❸ Divide the sweet red bean paste into 12 portions. Wrap a half salt-preserved egg yolk in each portion of bean paste (illus. 3).

❹ Roll out the pieces of dough once more, then wrap one portion of salt-preserved egg yolk and red bean paste in each. Arrange on a cookie sheet, and brush the top of each with some lightly beaten egg yolk. Garnish with sesame seeds (illus. 4). Bake at 180°C (360°F) until golden (about 20 minutes).

猪肉酥餅

Pork Pastries

材料：
外皮：與元寶酥相同（見第58頁）
內餡：

絞腿肉	300公克
葱花	$\frac{1}{2}$ 杯
大蒜酥	$\frac{1}{2}$ 杯
醬油	2大匙
香油	2大匙
太白粉	2大匙
糖	$\frac{1}{2}$ 小匙
鹽	$\frac{1}{4}$ 小匙
胡椒粉	少許
味精	少許

❶內餡材料加調味料拌勻（圖1），略爲冷凍。
❷外皮分成25等份，各包入1大匙內餡（圖2），略爲壓扁（圖3），入200℃（390°F）烤箱烤15分鐘，翻面再烤5分鐘即可（圖4）。

INGREDIENTS:
Dough: Same as for Silver Ingot Pastries
(p. 58).

Filling:

300g (⅔ lb.)	ground pork
½ c.	chopped green onion
½ c.	fried garlic flakes
2 T.	soy sauce
2 T.	sesame oil
2 T.	cornstarch
½ t.	sugar
¼ t.	salt
dash	white pepper

❶ Mix the filling ingredients and seasonings until blended (illus. 1). Freeze until partially solid.
❷ Divide the dough into 25 equally sized portions and wrap one tablespoon of meat filling in each (illus. 2). Lightly press each pastry flat (illus. 3). Bake on one side in a 200°C (390°F) oven for 15 minutes, then turn over the pastries and bake another 5 minutes (illus. 4).

蓮花酥餅

材料：
外皮

①	中筋麵粉 ……150公克 猪油………………37公克 熱開水 …………$\frac{1}{2}$杯 紅色6號…………少許	②	中筋麵粉 ……150公克 猪油…………………37公克 熱開水 …………$\frac{1}{2}$杯
內餡：蓮蓉 ……225公克		③	中筋麵粉 ……300公克 猪油 …………150公克

❶①、②、③料分別揉勻，①、②分成12等份，③分成24等份。

❷③作餡心，12等份分別包入①之麵皮內（圖1），其餘12等份再分別包入②之麵皮內。

❸以②、③作成之麵皮，包入1大匙內餡，再當餡心，包入以①、③作成之麵皮內，捏成圓形（圖2）。

❹將成品用刀片割成6瓣花瓣（圖3），放入4分熱油炸至皮酥即可（圖4）。

Lotus Pastries

INGREDIENTS:

Doughs:

①	150g (⅓ lb.)	all-purpose (medium gluten) flour
	37g (1⅓ oz.)	lard or shortening
	½ c.	boiling water
	few drops	red food coloring
②	150g (⅓ lb.)	all-purpose (medium gluten) flour
	37g (1⅓ oz.)	lard or shortening
	½ c.	boiling water
③	300g (⅔ lb.)	all-purpose (medium gluten) flour
	150g (⅓ lb.)	lard or shortening

Filling:

225g (½ lb.)   sweet lotus seed paste

❶ Mix the ingredients in ① , ② , and ③ separately. Divide doughs ① and ② into 12 equally sized pieces each. Divide dough ③ into 24 equally sized pieces.

❷ Wrap half the pieces of dough ③ in the pieces of dough①. Wrap the remaining pieces of dough ③ in the pieces of dough ② (illus. 1).

❸ Wrap one tablespoon of filling in the pieces of dough made from doughs ② and ③ . Then wrap each of these in a piece of the dough made from doughs ① and ③ . Pinch into round balls (illus. 2).

❹ With a single edge razor blade, carve out 6 petals in each pastry (illus. 3). Deep-fry in cooking oil over low to medium heat until crisp and flaky (illus. 4).

叉燒酥餅

材料：
外皮：與元寶酥相同（見第58頁）
內餡：叉燒肉 ……225公克
蛋黃 ………………………1個
香菜葉…………………………25葉

① 水 …………………………1杯
澄粉 …………………………1大匙
麵粉 …………………………1大匙
玉米粉 ………………………1大匙
太白粉 ………………………1大匙
醬油 …………………………1小匙
蠔油 …………………………1小匙
糖 ……………………………1小匙
鹽………………………………½ 小匙
味精…………………………… ⅛ 小匙

❶叉燒肉切成小細丁，①料煮開待凉，與叉燒肉拌勻（圖1）。

❷外皮分成25等份，每份包入內餡後略爲壓扁（圖2），表面塗上蛋黃後（圖3），粘上一片香菜葉作裝飾（圖4），入200℃（390°F）烤箱烤至金黃色即可。

Roast Pork Pastries

INGREDIENTS:
Dough: Same as for Silver Ingot Pastries (p. 58).

Filling:

225g (½ lb.)		Cantonese style roast pork *(cha siu)*
①	1 c.	water
	2 T.	cornstarch
	1 T.	wheat starch
	1 T.	flour
	1 t.	soy sauce
	1 t.	oyster sauce
	1 t.	sugar
	½ t.	salt
1		egg yolk
25 leaves		fresh coriander

❶ Dice the Cantonese style roast pork. Bring ① to boil in a saucepan or wok, then allow to cool. Stir in the diced pork (illus. 1).

❷ Divide the dough into 25 equally sized portions. Wrap some filling in each piece of dough and lightly flatten (illus. 2). Brush some lightly beaten egg yolk over the tops (illus. 3). Place one coriander leaf on the top of each as a garnish (illus. 4). Bake in a 200°C (390°F) oven until golden.

鴛鴦酥盒

材料：
外皮：與元寶酥同（見第58頁）
內餡：

白蘿蔔絲 ……………600公克

① 蝦米 …………… $\frac{1}{4}$ 杯
葱花 …………… $\frac{1}{4}$ 杯
肥豬油丁 …………… $\frac{1}{4}$ 杯
香油 …………… 2大匙
味精 …………… $\frac{1}{2}$ 小匙
鹽 …………… $\frac{1}{2}$ 小匙
胡椒粉 …………… 少許

豆沙 ………………………半斤
蛋黃 ………………………1個
鹽 ………………………2大匙

❶ 外皮折3折後，再一分爲二（圖1）。
❷ 白蘿蔔絲先用2大匙鹽醃軟後，使用清水將鹹味洗掉，並擠乾水分。
❸ 將蘿蔔絲及①料拌勻，是爲蘿蔔餡。
❹ 外皮捍薄後一半包蘿蔔餡、一半包豆沙餡，各捏成半月形（圖2），再將兩個半月形粘貼成一個圓形，並捏花邊（圖3）。
❺ 包豆沙餡的一邊，上塗蛋黃，續入 200℃（390℉）烤箱烤至金黃色即可（約20分鐘）。

INGREDIENTS:
Dough: Same as for Silver Ingot Pastries (p. 58).

Filling I:

600g (1 lb. 5 oz.)	Chinese white radish (daikon), grated
¼ c.	dried shrimps
¼ c.	chopped green onion
¼ c.	fat pork, diced
2 T.	sesame oil
½ t.	salt
pinch	white pepper

Filling II:

300g (⅔ lb.)	sweet red bean paste
1	egg yolk
2 T.	salt

❶ Fold the sheet of dough into thirds, then cut into halves (illus. 1).
❷ Mix 2 tablespoons salt into the grated Chinese white radish and allow to set until soft. Rinse under tap water to wash away the salt, then squeeze out the excess moisture.
❸ Mix the grated Chinese white radish together with the rest of the ingredients for filling I.
❹ Roll out each piece of dough into a thin sheet. Wrap the radish filling in one sheet, and the sweet red bean paste in the other, pinching each into a crescent shape as illustrated (illus. 2). Pinch the two crescent shapes into a circle shape and flute the edges (illus. 3).
❺ Brush some lightly beaten egg yolk on the red bean paste side. Bake in a 200°C (390°F) oven until golden brown, about 20 minutes.

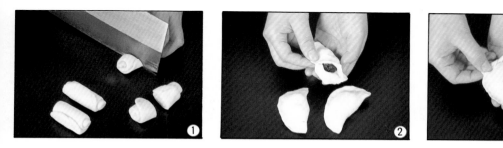

椰子餅

Coconut Bars

材料：
外皮：
低筋麵粉 ……………… 300公克
糖粉 ………………… 112公克
酥油 …………………… 75公克
蛋 …………………………… 1個
奶水 ……………………… 3大匙
內餡：
椰子粉 ………………… 225公克
糖 …………………… 150公克
奶油……………………… 75公克
奶水 ……………………… 37公克
蛋 …………………………… 1個

❶外皮材料揉成麵糰後，提成20×30公分的薄皮（圖1
），放入適當大小的烤盤裡。
❷內餡材料揉拌均勻。
❸將內餡均勻地舖於麵皮上（圖2），入烤箱上火180°
C（360°F）、下火200°C（390°F），烤至金黃色即可。
■入烤箱前先用牙籤刺穿（圖3），以便空氣排出。

INGREDIENTS:
Dough:

300g (²⁄₃ lb.)	low gluten (cake) flour
112g (¼ lb.)	sugar
75g (2²⁄₃ oz.)	shortening
1	egg
3 T.	evaporated milk

Filling:

225g (½ lb.)	desiccated (or flaked) coconut
150g (⅓ lb.)	sugar (use less sugar if using sweetened coconut)
75g (2²⁄₃ oz.)	butter
37g (1¹⁄₃ oz.)	evaporated milk
1	egg

❶ Mix the dough ingredients and knead. Roll out into a 20 x 30cm (8″ x 12″) sheet (illus. 1). Transfer to a cookie sheet.
❷ Mix the filling ingredients until well combined.
❸ Spread the filling over the sheet of dough (illus. 2). Bake in a 180°C (360°F) oven until golden.

■ Pierce several times with a toothpick before baking to allow steam to escape (illus. 3).

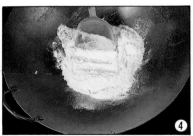

椒鹽芝蔴酥

材料：

外皮：與元寶酥相同（見第 58 頁）

內餡：

| 黑、白芝蔴 ……………各75公克 | 糖、熟麵粉…………各150公克 |
| 鹽………………………1小匙 | 豬油…………………………75公克 |

❶將中筋麵粉用小火炒至微黃色即爲熟麵粉（圖4）。

❷黑、白芝蔴洗淨後，用中火炒熟，趁熱略爲壓碎（圖5）。再加入其它配料拌匀即爲內餡。

❸外皮分爲25等份，每份包 1 小匙內餡，略爲壓扁（圖6），入180℃（360°F）烤箱烤15分鐘，翻面再烤5分鐘即可。

Sesame Pastries

INGREDIENTS:

Dough: Same as for Silver Ingot Pastries (p. 58).

Filling:

75g (2⅔ oz.) each:	black and white sesame seeds
1 t.	salt
150g (⅓ lb.) each:	sugar, flour
75g (2⅔ oz.)	lard or shortening

❶ Roast the flour in a dry wok over low heat until lightly golden (illus. 4).

❷ Wash the white and black sesame seeds and drain. Toast them in a dry wok over medium heat until the white sesame seeds are lightly golden. Grind while hot into a powder (illus. 5). Mix in the remaining ingredients to form the filling.

❸ Divide the dough into 25 equally sized pieces. Wrap one teaspoon of filling in each piece of dough and press lightly to flatten (illus. 6). Arrange on a cookie sheet and bake in a 180°C (360°F) oven for 15 minutes. Turn over the pastries and bake another 5 minutes.

蛋 塔

Custard Tarts

材料：

外皮：

《水油皮》

		內餡：	
中筋麵粉	……150公克	水	……………300公克
水	…………75公克	糖	……………150公克
油	…………37公克	蛋	………………5個
奶水	…………18公克	蛋塔模型	…………12個
糖	……………2大匙	蛋黃	………………1個

《油酥》

中筋麵粉 ……112公克

油 …………75公克

❶ 外皮作法與蛋黃酥相同（見第 60 頁），擀開後放入蛋塔模型中（圖1），周圍摺出花紋（圖2），並在花紋上塗少許蛋黃液（圖3）。

❷ 糖與水煮溶後放涼，再打入蛋液拌勻，即為內餡。

❸ 將蛋液倒入模型內，入烤箱，上火160°C（320°F），下火200°C（390°F），烤至周圍蛋黃略為變色時，以鐵盤蓋住蛋塔，熄火，燜至蛋黃液凝固即可。

INGREDIENTS:

Water-shortening dough:

150g (⅓ lb.)	all-purpose (medium gluten) flour	
75g (2½ oz.)	water	
37g (1⅓ oz.)	cooking oil	
18g (⅔ oz.)	evaporated milk	
2 T.	sugar	

Flaky dough:

112g (¼ lb.)	all-purpose (medium gluten) flour
75g (2½ oz.)	cooking oil

Filling:

5	eggs
300g (⅔ lb.)	water
150g (⅓ lb.)	sugar
12	tart molds
1	egg yolk

❶ Make the crust according to the same method as for Egg Yolk-Red Bean Pastries (p.60). Roll out the crust, then fit into the tart molds (illus. 1). Flute the edges (illus. 2). Brush some beaten egg yolk over the fluted edges (illus. 3).

❷ Bring the sugar and water to a boil. Cook until the sugar is thoroughly dissolved, then allow to cool. Beat the eggs and stir into the sugar water until blended.

❸ Pour the egg mixture into the dough-lined tart molds. Place in an oven preheated to 180°C (360°F). Bake until the egg yolk on the edges turns yellow, then cover the tarts with a metal cookie sheet. Turn off the heat and leave in the oven until the custard is firm.

油炸酥餅

材料：

外皮：《水油皮》　　《油酥》　　　　　內餡：

中筋麵粉…300公克　低筋麵粉……225公克　白豆沙……300公克

豬油………75公克　豬油…………112公克　碎桔餅……150公克

熱開水………$\frac{3}{4}$杯　　　　　　　　　熟白芝蔴……75公克

❶將水油皮、油酥分別揉勻，切成30等份，油酥包在水油皮內，提開後
折3折（圖4），作2次。

❷內餡材料揉勻。

❸取1份麵皮提薄後，包入1大匙內餡，包成半月形（圖5），邊緣捏出
花邊（圖6）。

❹炸油燒6分熟（約120℃，250°F），入鍋炸至金黃色即可。

Deep-Fried Kumquat Pastries

INGREDIENTS:

Water-shortening dough:

300g (⅔ lb.)	all-purpose (medium gluten) flour
75g (2⅔ oz.)	lard or shortening
¾ c.	boiling water

Flaky dough:

| 225g (½ lb.) | low gluten (cake) flour |
| 112g (¼ lb.) | lard or shortening |

Filling:

300g (⅔ lb.)	sweet kidney bean paste
150g (⅓ lb.)	minced candied kumquats
75g (2⅔ oz.)	toasted white sesame seeds

❶ Mix the ingredients for the water-shortening dough and the flaky dough
separately. Divide both types of dough into 30 pieces each. Wrap the
pieces of flaky dough inside the pieces of water-shortening dough. Roll
out and fold into thirds twice (illus. 4).

❷ Mix the filling ingredients together until well combined.

❸ Roll out a portion of dough and wrap one tablespoon of filling in it. Form
into a cresent shape (illus. 5), fluting the edges (illus. 6).

❹ Heat oil for frying to 120°C (250°F) and deep-fry the pastries until golden.

核桃酥

材料：

外皮：與元寶酥相同（見第58頁）

內餡：

核桃	⋯⋯⋯150公克	奶油	⋯⋯⋯37公克
熟麵粉	⋯⋯⋯150公克	奶水	⋯⋯⋯37公克
細糖	⋯⋯⋯112公克	蛋黃	⋯⋯⋯1個

❶核桃用7分熱油（約140℃，280°F）炸熟，略爲切碎後（圖1），和其它材料拌匀成內餡。

❷外皮提薄，包入1大匙內餡（圖2），略壓扁（圖3），在表面塗上蛋黃，入200℃（390°F）烤箱烤至金黃。

Walnut Pastries

INGREDIENTS:

Dough: Same as for Silver Ingot Pastries (p. 58).

Filling:

150g (⅓ lb.)	walnuts
150g (⅓ lb.)	roasted flour
112g (¼ lb.)	sugar
37g (1⅓ oz.)	butter
37g (1⅓ oz.)	evaporated milk
1	egg yolk

❶ Deep-fry the walnuts briefly in cooking oil heated to 140°C (280°F), being careful not to burn them. Chop coarsely (illus. 1). Mix with the other filling ingredients until well combined.

❷ Roll out each piece of dough until thin. Wrap one tablespoon of filling inside each (illus. 2) and flatten lightly (illus. 3). Brush some lightly beaten egg yolk on each and arrange on a cookie sheet. Bake in a 200°C (390°F) oven until golden.

菊花酥餅

材料：

外皮：與元寶酥相同　　　　蛋黃 ⋯⋯⋯⋯⋯1個
　　　（見第58頁）　　　　黑芝蔴⋯⋯⋯⋯⋯少許

內餡：棗泥⋯⋯⋯300公克

❶每份外皮，包入2小匙棗泥餡（圖4），再壓平，用小刀切出菊花瓣（圖5），續在中央部份塗上蛋黃並灑上數粒芝蔴做花蕊（圖6）。

❷烤箱熱至上火180℃（360°F）、下火200℃（390°F），放入菊花酥烤15分鐘即可。

Chrysanthemum Pastries

INGREDIENTS:

Dough: Same as for Silver Ingot Pastries (p. 58).

Filling:

300g (⅔ lb.)	Chinese date paste
1	egg yolk
as needed	black sesame seeds

❶ Wrap two teaspoons of Chinese date paste in each piece of dough (illus. 4), then flatten. Carve out chrysanthemum petals with a small knife (illus. 5). Brush some lightly beaten egg yolk on the center of each and sprinkle on some black sesame seeds for the pollen (illus. 6).

❷ Preheat the oven to 180°C (360°F). Arrange the chrysanthemum pastries on a baking sheet and bake 15 minutes.

花生酥餅

材料：
外皮：與元寶酥相同（見第 58 頁）
內餡：

花生粉	1杯	沙拉油	$\frac{1}{2}$杯
細糖	$\frac{1}{2}$杯	鷄蛋	1個
熟麵粉	$\frac{1}{2}$杯	蛋黃	1個

❶先將內餡材料揉匀備用。
❷外皮分成25等份，每份包入1大匙內餡後，提成長方形（圖7），約在
　中央用刀割一個3公分的刀口（圖8），續將兩頭倒轉成繩索狀（圖9）
❸將作好之成品表面塗蛋黃，入200℃（390°F）烤箱，烤至金黃色即可。

Peanut Pastries

INGREDIENTS:
Dough: Same as for Silver Ingot Pastries (p. 58).

Filling:

1 c.	peanut powder
½ c.	sugar
½ c.	roasted flour
½ c.	cooking oil
1	egg
1	egg yolk

❶ Mix the filling ingredients until well blended.
❷ Divide the dough into 25 equally sized portions. Wrap one tablespoon of filling in each piece of dough and roll it out into a
rectangular shape (illus.7). With a knife, make a 3cm (1¼″) slash
on the top center of each (illus.8). Flute the two edges of the slash
on each pastry to form a ropelike pattern (illus.9).
❸ Brush some lightly beaten egg yolk over the top of each pastry.
Bake in a 200°C (390°F) oven until golden.

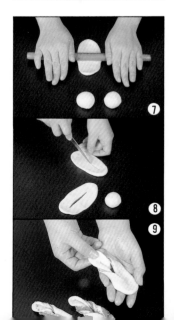

甘露酥

材料：

外皮：

低筋麵粉	……300公克
糖	……112公克
豬油	……112公克
蛋	……2個
軟凍粉	……2大匙
蘇打粉	……½小匙

內餡：

黑豆沙	……300公克
蛋黃	……2個

❶ 將外皮材料揉勻後，提成8×50公分之薄皮。
❷ 豆沙亦揉搓成50公分之長條狀(圖1)。
❸ 將豆沙置於外皮上，捲成長方條，略整爲四方形後(圖2)，在表面塗上蛋黃(圖3)，入200℃(390°F)烤箱烤至金黃色取出待涼，切成25小塊即可。

Red Bean Pastries

INGREDIENTS:

Dough:

300g (⅔ lb.)	low gluten (cake) flour
112g (¼ lb.)	sugar
112g (¼ lb.)	lard or shortening
2	eggs
2 T.	custard powder
½ t.	baking soda

Filling:

300g (⅔ lb.)	sweet red bean paste
2	egg yolks

❶ Mix the dough ingredients together and knead. Roll out into a thin 8 x 50cm (3″ x 20″) strip.
❷ Press the sweet red bean paste into a 50cm (20″) long strip (illus. 1).
❸ Place the strip of bean paste on the dough and roll into a rectangular shape. Form into a roughly square shape (illus. 2). Brush some lightly beaten egg yolk over the top (illus. 3). Bake in a 200°C (390°F) oven until golden. Remove from oven and allow to cool. Cut into 25 pieces.

❶

❷

❸

翡翠芝蔴捲

材料：

外皮：
糯米粉 ·········150公克
菠菜 ··········150公克
太白粉··········75公克
水 ·············$1\frac{1}{2}$杯

內餡：
熟白芝蔴 ··········1杯
細糖··············$\frac{1}{2}$杯

❶ 菠菜加水用果汁機打碎過濾（圖1），濾水加入糯米粉、太白粉拌勻，再倒入塗油的平盤內，約0.3公分厚度。

❷ 將平盤放入蒸鍋內，大火蒸5分鐘，取出放涼。

❸ 白芝蔴炒熟，趁熱搗碎（圖2），並加入糖拌勻。

❹ 將芝蔴粉均勻地灑於粿粉皮上，捲起成圓筒狀（圖3），再切成4公分長段即可。

Emerald Sesame Rolls

INGREDIENTS:

Dough:
150g (⅓ lb.)	glutinous rice (mochi) flour
150g (⅓ lb.)	fresh spinach
75g (2⅔ oz.)	cornstarch
1½ c.	water

Filling:
1 c.	white sesame seeds
½ c.	sugar

❶ Puree the fresh, washed spinach in a blender with the water. Pour into a strainer, saving the liquid (illus. 1). Add the strained liquid to the glutinous rice flour and the cornstarch, and mix well. Pour into an oiled cakepan to a thickness of about 0.3cm (⅛″).

❷ Place the cakepan in a steamer and steam over high heat for 5 minutes. Remove from the steamer and allow to cool.

❸ Toast the sesame seeds by stir-frying in a dry wok. Pound into a powder (iilus. 2). Mix in the sugar.

❹ Sprinkle the sweet sesame powder evenly over the steamed rice cake, then roll into a cylindrical shape (illus. 3). Cut into 4cm (1½″) pieces.

廣式蘿蔔糕

材料：
①	在來米 ……480公克		③	鹽 ……………1大匙
	蓬萊米 ……120公克			胡椒粉 ………1小匙
白蘿蔔絲 ……1200公克				味精 …………1小匙
②	臘腸………95公克		沙拉油 …………7大匙
	紅葱頭………95公克			
	蝦米…………37公克			

❶①料洗淨加水泡約12小時後，瀝乾，再加3杯水，用果汁機拌打成米漿（圖1）。

❷4大匙沙拉油炒軟白蘿蔔絲後，取出備用。

❸蝦米洗淨切細，臘腸切0.5公分小丁，紅葱頭切細末（圖2）備用。

❹油3大匙，炒香2料，再放入③料和已炒軟的蘿蔔絲拌勻（圖3），熄火後倒入米漿拌勻（圖4），入蒸鍋大火蒸1小時即可。

Cantonese White Radish Cake

INGREDIENTS:
①	480g (1 lb., 1 oz.)	long grain white rice
	120g (¼ lb.)	short grain white rice
1200g (2⅔ lb.)		Chinese white radish (daikon), shredded
②	95g (3⅓ oz.)	Chinese sausage
	95g (3⅓ oz.)	shallots
	37g (1⅓ oz.)	dried shrimp
③	1 T.	salt
	1 t.	white pepper
7 T.		cooking oil

❶ Wash the two kinds of rice, add three cups water, and soak for 12 hours. Liquefy in a blender (illus. 1).

❷ Stir-fry the shredded Chinese white radish in 4 tablespoons cooking oil until soft. Remove from wok or pan.

❸ Wash the dried shrimp and mince. Cut the Chinese sausage into 0.5cm (¼") cubes. Mince the shallots (illus. 2).

❹ Fry ② until fragrant in 3 tablespoons cooking oil, then add ③ and the stir-fried shredded Chinese white radish until well combined (illus. 3). Turn off the heat and mix in the liquefied rice (illus. 4). Place in a steamer and steam over high heat for one hour. Slice to serve. The slices may also be pan-fried.

地瓜肉丸

Sweet Potato Meat Balls

材料：
外皮：
去皮地瓜 ……600公克
太白粉 ………225公克
細糖………75公克
沙拉油 ………1大匙
鹽………½小匙

內餡：
後腿肉(切丁)‥200公克
香菇(切丁)………10朵
熟竹筍(切丁) ……1支
熟栗子…………15粒
① { 水 ………2大匙
太白粉、麵粉………
…………各1大匙
鹽 …………1小匙
味精 …………¼小匙
胡椒粉、酒…各少許
沙拉油 ………1½大匙

沾料：
細糖 ………112公克
味噌…………75公克
番茄醬 ………75公克
水 …………1杯
蠔油 …………2小匙
辣油 …………1小匙
香油 …………1小匙
味精…………¼小匙
② { 水 …………3大匙
元宵粉 ……2大匙
香菜…………… 1杯

❶鍋燒熱，入1½大匙沙拉油內餡材料及①料炒熟放涼。

❷地瓜切片蒸熟(約20分鐘)，加入其它材料揉勻（圖1），並分成15等份。

❸每份地瓜包入1½大匙內餡（圖2），入蒸籠大火蒸10分鐘取出。

❹沾料煮開後，用②料芶芡，淋於肉圓上（圖3），並灑上香菜即可。

INGREDIENTS:
Dough:
600g (1⅓ lb.)	sweet potatoes, pared
225g (½ lb.)	cornstarch
75g (2⅔ oz.)	sugar
1 T.	cooking oil
½ t.	salt

Filling:
200g (7 oz.)	pork (hind leg meat), diced
10	dried Chinese black mushrooms, soaked until soft and diced
1	fresh bamboo shoot, cooked and diced
15	chestnuts
① { 2 T.	water
1 T. each:	cornstarch, flour
1 t.	salt
dash each:	white pepper, rice wine
1½ T.	cooking oil

Dip:
112g (¼ lb.)	sugar
75g (2⅔ oz.)	miso
75g (2⅔ oz.)	ketchup
1 c.	water
2 t.	oyster sauce
1 t.	chili oil
1 t.	sesame oil
② { 3 T.	water
2 T.	glutinous rice flour
1 c.	fresh coriander (Chinese parsley)

❶ Preheat a wok and add 1½ tablespoons oil. Stir-fry the filling ingredients with ① until cooked through. Allow to cool.

❷ Slice the sweet potatoes and steam until soft, about 20 minutes. Add the other dough ingredients and knead until smooth (illus. 1). Divide into 15 equally sized portions.

❸ Fill each portion of sweet potato dough with 1½ tablespoons filling (illus. 2). Arrange in a steamer and steam over high heat for 10 minutes. Remove from steamer.

❹ Bring the dip ingredients to a boil, thicken with ②, and drizzle over the sweet potato meat balls (illus. 3). Sprinkle a little chopped fresh coriander over the top.

水蒸蛋糕

材料：

鷄蛋	750公克
細糖	450公克
低筋麵粉	450公克
冬瓜糖（切碎）	225公克
沙拉油	$\frac{1}{2}$ 杯
奶水	$\frac{1}{2}$ 杯
軟凍粉	4大匙
黑芝蔴	2大匙
泡打粉	1大匙
香草片	6片
玻璃紙	1張

❶將蛋黃、蛋白分開後，蛋黃與油、奶水、香草、冬瓜糖、軟凍粉拌勻，即爲蛋黃液。

❷低筋麵粉與泡打粉過篩（圖1）。

❸蛋白打發泡後（圖2），糖分3次加入打散，再加入蛋黃液和麵粉拌勻，最後倒入舖好玻璃紙的容器中（圖3）（麵糊高度約4公分），上灑黑芝蔴、大火蒸30分鐘，取出切塊即可。

Steamed Cake

INGREDIENTS:

750g (1$\frac{2}{3}$ lb.)	eggs
450g (1 lb.)	sugar
450g (1 lb.)	low gluten (cake) flour
225g ($\frac{1}{2}$ lb.)	wintermelon candy, minced
$\frac{1}{2}$ c.	cooking oil
$\frac{1}{2}$ c.	evaporated milk
4 T.	custard powder
2 T.	black sesame seeds
1 T.	baking powder
1 sheet	cellophane
$\frac{1}{8}$ t.	vanilla extract

❶ Separate the egg yolks and whites. Mix the oil, evaporated milk, vanilla extract, wintermelon candy, and custard powder with the egg yolks until well combined.

❷ Sift the flour and baking powder together (illus. 1).

❸ Beat the egg whites until foamy (illus. 2). Beat in the sugar, one third at a time, beating well after each addition. Stir in the egg yolk mixture and flour-baking powder mixture. Pour into a cellophane-lined container (illus. 3). (The batter should be about 4cm or 1$\frac{1}{2}$" high.) Sprinkle the black sesame seeds over the top, then steam for 30 minutes. Remove from the steamer and cut.

炸芝蔴球

材料：

元宵粉	300公克	熱開水	$1\frac{1}{2}$ 杯
澄粉	37公克	棗泥	225公克
豬油	2大匙	白芝蔴	1杯
細糖	1大匙		

❶元宵粉、澄粉、糖及豬油先拌勻，再用 $1\frac{1}{2}$ 杯熱開水拌揉成燙麵糰（圖4），分成16等份。

❷每份麵皮包入1小匙棗泥餡（圖5），再用清水略為沾濕，並沾裹芝蔴（圖6），再入5分熱油（約95°C，200°F）炸至金黃色即可。

Sesame Balls

INGREDIENTS:

300g (2/3 lb.)	glutinous rice (mochi) flour
225g (1/2 lb.)	Chinese date paste
37g (1 1/3 oz.)	wheat starch
1 c.	white sesame seeds
2 T.	lard
1 T.	sugar
1 1/2 c.	boiling water

❶ Mix the glutinous rice flour, wheat starch, sugar, and lard until well combined. Add 1½ cups water and knead into a smooth dough (illus. 4). Divide into 16 equally sized portions.

❷ Wrap one teaspoon of Chinese date paste filling in each portion of dough (illus. 5). Dip each into water to moisten, then roll in the white sesame seeds (illus.6). Deep fry in oil heated to about 95°C (200°F) until golden.

紅豆鬆糕

材料：
在來米粉 ··················225公克
細糖 ··················187公克
水 ··················112公克
紅豆··················75公克
糯米粉··················75公克
白紙 ··················1張

❶紅豆洗淨，泡水6小時，再放入電鍋蒸爛（約1小時），取出倒去湯汁，加入75公克細糖拌勻放涼。

❷在來米粉與糯米粉先拌均勻。

❸112公克細糖先溶於水中，再灑入米粉（圖1），揉搓成細粉狀。

❹白紙墊於蒸籠裡（圖2），先鋪上半量米粉，再灑上紅豆，最後再灑上半量米粉（圖3），入蒸鍋大火蒸30分鐘取出切塊即可。

Red Bean Rice Cake

INGREDIENTS:

225g (½ lb.)	long grain rice flour (not glutinous)
187g (6½ oz.)	sugar
112g (¼ lb.)	water
75g (2⅔ oz.)	glutinous rice (mochi) flour
75g (2⅔ oz.)	red (adzuki) beans
1 sheet	white paper

❶ Wash the red beans thoroughly, then soak in cold water for 6 hours. Steam in an electric rice cooker or steamer until soft, about one hour. Remove from the steamer and pour off the liquid. Stir in 75g (2⅔ oz.) sugar until dissolved, then allow to cool.

❷ Mix the plain rice flour and glutinous rice flour together until well combined.

❸ Dissolve 112g (¼ lb.) sugar in the water, then add the mixed rice flour (illus. 1). Mix to form a fine powder.

❹ Line a steamer with the white paper (illus. 2). Pour on half of the rice powder, then sprinkle on the red beans, and finally cover with the rest of the rice powder (illus. 3). Steam over high heat for 30 minutes. Remove and cut in rectangles.

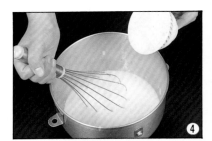

馬拉糕

材料：

鶏蛋	400公克	中筋麵粉	250公克
砂糖	200公克	多瓜糖	100公克
沙拉油	4大匙	泡打粉	$\frac{1}{4}$大匙
奶水	2大匙	玻璃紙	1張
		黑芝蔴	少許

❶多瓜糖切碎。

❷鶏蛋打入鋼盆裡，打至發泡後加入半量砂糖（圖4）打至溶解。

❸沙拉油、奶水、泡打粉、中筋麵粉及砂糖一起倒入發泡之蛋液中（圖5）拌匀、再拌入多瓜糖即爲蛋糕。

❹取一容器，舖上玻璃紙，再倒入蛋糕（圖6），上灑黑芝蔴，入蒸鍋大火蒸40分鐘即可。

Chinese Sponge Cake

INGREDIENTS:

400g (14 oz.)	eggs
250g (9 oz.)	all-purpose (medium gluten) flour
200g (7 oz.)	sugar
100g (3½ oz.)	wintermelon candy
4 T.	cooking oil
2 T.	evaporated milk
¼ T.	baking powder
1 sheet	cellophane
as needed	black sesame seeds

❶ Mince the wintermelon candy.

❷ Beat the eggs until foamy. Add half of the sugar (illus. 4) and beat until dissolved.

❸ Mix the cooking oil, evaporated milk, baking powder, flour, and sugar until blended. Add to the egg mixture (illus. 5), then fold in the minced wintermelon candy.

❹ Line a cake pan with cellophane and pour in the batter (illus. 6). Sprinkle the black sesame seeds over the top. Place in a steamer and steam over high heat for 40 minutes.

芋頭糕

Taro Cake

材料：

芋頭	…………300公克		香油	…………3大匙
在來米粉	………300公克		細糖	…………2小匙
澄粉	…………37公克	①	鹽	…………1小匙
太白粉	…………37公克		味精	…………$\frac{1}{2}$小匙
油葱酥	…………3大匙			
芹菜末	…………3大匙			

❶芋頭去皮後切成絲，用7分熱油(約140℃，280°F)炸熟（圖1）備用。

❷在來米粉、澄粉、太白粉及①料等先用1杯半溫開水調開（圖2），再沖入2杯半的滾開水使成麵糊。

❸麵糊中加入芋頭絲拌勻，倒入擦油的容器裡，上灑油葱酥（圖3），再入蒸鍋大火蒸40分鐘，取出再灑上芹菜末即可。

INGREDIENTS:

300g (2/3 lb.)	taros
300g (2/3 lb.)	long grain rice flour (not glutinous)
37g (1 1/3 oz.)	wheat starch
37g (1 1/3 oz.)	cornstarch
3 T.	fried green onion flakes
3 T.	minced Chinese celery

	3 T.	sesame oil
①	2 t.	sugar
	1 t.	salt

❶ Pare the taros and cut into julienne strips or grate coarsely. Deep-fry in oil heated to about 140°C (280°F) until done (illus. 1).

❷ Combine the long grain rice flour, wheat starch, cornstarch, and ① . Mix into a paste after adding 1½ cups of warm water (illus. 2), then add 2½ cups of boiling water to form a batter.

❸ Add the taro slivers to the batter and mix well. Pour into an oiled container, and sprinkle the fried green onion flakes over the top (illus. 3). Place in a steamer and steam over high heat for 40 minutes. Sprinkle the minced Chinese celery over the top.

地瓜花生糯糕

材料：

外皮：
　元宵粉 ……………………300公克
　熱開水 ……………………1½杯
　沙拉油 ……………………2大匙

內餡：
　去皮地瓜 …………………300公克
　花生粉 ……………………150公克
　細糖 ………………………112公克
　沙拉油 ……………………3大匙

❶外皮揉勻成麵糰，分成20等份。
❷地瓜蒸熟後趁熱搗碎（圖4），並加入糖、沙拉油拌勻成內餡（圖5）。
❸每份外皮包入1大匙內餡，入蒸鍋大火蒸6分鐘取出，趁熱沾裹花生粉（圖6）即可。

Sweet Potato Peanut Mochi

INGREDIENTS:
Dough:
300g (²⁄₃ lb.)	glutinous rice flour
1½ c.	boiling water
2 T.	cooking oil

Filling:
300g (²⁄₃ lb.)	sweet potatoes or yams, pared
112g (¼ lb.)	sugar
3 T.	cooking oil
150g (¹⁄₃ lb.)	peanut powder

❶ Knead the dough ingredients until smooth. Divide into 20 equally sized portions.
❷ Steam the sweet potatoes or yams until soft. Mash until smooth while still hot (illus. 4). Mix in the sugar and cooking oil to form the filling (illus. 5).
❸ Wrap one tablespoon filling inside each portion of dough. Arrange in a steamer and steam over high heat for 6 minutes. Remove from the steamer, and roll in the peanut powder while still hot (illus. 6).

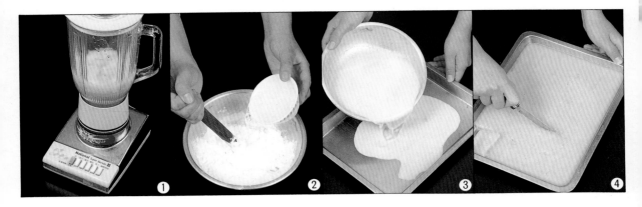

鳳梨軟糕

Pineapple Dessert

材料：

鳳梨罐頭	1罐
細糖	112公克
椰子粉	100公克
澄粉	75公克
玉米粉	37公克
太白粉	37公克
水	$1\frac{1}{2}$ 杯

❶將鳳梨和汁一起用果汁機打碎（圖1）。

❷太白粉、玉米粉和澄粉先用1杯水調開爲粉水（圖2）。

❸將鳳梨肉汁倒入鍋中，加糖和半杯水煮開後，續入粉水拌勻成糊狀，再倒入擦油的平底容器中（圖3）（厚約2.5公分），入蒸鍋大火蒸10分鐘，取出放凉，切成 所須大小（圖4），沾上椰子粉即可。

INGREDIENTS:

1 can	pineapple
112g (¼ lb.)	sugar
100g (3½ oz.)	desiccated or flaked coconut
75g (2⅔ oz.)	wheat starch
75g (2⅔ oz.)	cornstarch
1½ c.	water

❶ Puree the pineapple with its syrup in a blender (illus. 1).

❷ Dissolve the cornstarch and wheat starch in a cup of water (illus. 2).

❸ Pour the pineapple puree into a pot, add the sugar and half a cup of water, and bring to a boil. Pour in the cornstarch-wheat starch water to thicken. Then pour the mixture into an oiled cake pan (illus. 3) to a thickness of about 2.5cm (1″). Place in a steamer and steam over high heat for 10 minutes. Remove and allow to cool. Cut into desired size pieces (illus. 4) and roll in desiccated or flaked coconut.

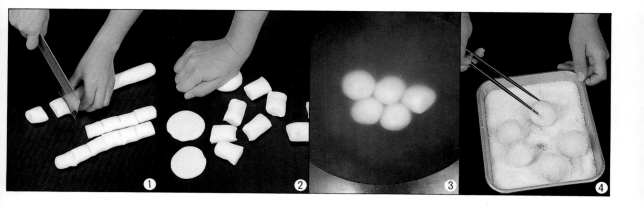

椰蓉糯米球

材料：

外皮：

元宵粉 …………………300公克
熱開水 …………………$1\frac{1}{2}$ 杯

內餡：

椰子粉 …………………150公克
細糖 ……………………75公克
奶油 ……………………37公克
雞蛋 ……………………1個
椰子粉 …………………75公克
櫻桃 ……………………1顆

❶外皮材料揉勻，分成20等份（圖1）。

❷內餡材料揉勻，略冰凍。

❸每份外皮稍壓扁（圖2），包入1大匙內餡，即為糯米球。

❹水煮開，入糯米球煮5分鐘，見膨脹（圖3）後撈起，趁熱放入椰子粉中沾裹均勻（圖4）排盤，上飾以切碎的櫻桃即可。

Coconut Balls

INGREDIENTS:

Dough:

| 300g (²/₃ lb.) | glutinous rice (mochi) flour |
| 1½ c. | boiling water |

Filling:

150g (¹/₃ lb.)	desiccated (or flaked) coconut
75g (2²/₃ oz.)	sugar (less if using sweetened coconut)
37g (1¹/₃ oz.)	butter
1	egg
75g (2²/₃ oz.)	desiccated (or flaked) coconut
1	maraschino cherry

❶ Knead the dough ingredients until smooth. Divide Into 20 equally sized portions (illus. 1).

❷ Mix the filling ingredients until well combined. Freeze until partially solid.

❸ Press each portion of dough flat (illus. 2), then wrap one tablespoon filling inside of each.

❹ Bring a pot of water to a boil. Drop in the coconut balls and cook for 5 minutes. Remove from the boiling water after they have expanded in volume (illus. 3). Roll in the desiccated coconut while hot, coating evenly (illus. 4). Arrange on a plate and garnish each with a bit of maraschino cherry.

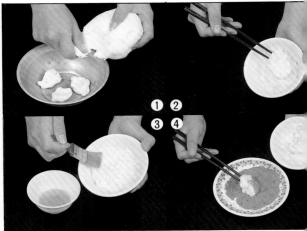

可可糯米粿

材料：

糯米粉	300公克	熱開水	$1\frac{3}{4}$杯
豆沙	225公克	可可粉	1大匙
麵粉	75公克	櫻桃	8粒
花生油	1大匙		

❶糯米粉加麵粉、可可粉拌勻，再加熱開水拌揉成麵糰後，分成16等份（圖1）。

❷將每份麵皮提開，包入1小匙豆沙餡（圖2），做成可可狀。

❸櫻桃對切，飾於可可粿上（圖3），入蒸籠大火蒸6分鐘取出，塗上花生油（圖4），以防沾粘即可。

Cocoa Rice Balls

INGREDIENTS:

300g (2/3 lb.)	glutinous rice (mochi) flour
225g (1/2 lb.)	sweet red bean paste
75g (2/3 oz.)	flour
1 3/4 c.	boiling water
1 T. each:	cocoa powder, peanut oil
8	maraschino cherries

❶ Mix together the glutinous rice flour, flour, and cocoa until well combined. Pour in the boiling water and knead into a dough. Divide into 16 equally sized portions (illus. 1).

❷ Roll each portion of dough flat, then wrap 1 teaspoon of sweet red bean paste filling in each (illus. 2).

❸ Halve the maraschino cherries and use to garnish the cocoa rice balls (illus. 3). Arrange in a steamer and steam over high heat for 6 minutes. Remove from the steamer and brush some peanut oil over each one to prevent sticking (illus. 4).

花生糍糬

材料：

糯米漿糰	600公克	細糖	112公克
花生粉	225公克		

❶糯米漿糰剝小塊（圖1），放入開水中煮熟撈起，並置於塗有花生油的容器內，趁熱用麵棍攪成很有韌性的麵糰（圖2），並在表面塗上少許沙拉油（圖3），以防風乾。

❷花生粉和細糖拌勻。

❸食時，捏起所要的份量，沾上花生粉即可（圖4）。

■此即本省聞名之客家糍糬。

Peanut Mochi

INGREDIENTS:

600g (1 1/3 lb.)	glutinous rice (mochi) flour dough
225g (1/2 lb.)	peanut powder
112g (1/4 lb.)	sugar

❶ Break the glutinous rice flour dough into small pieces (illus. 1). Place in boiling water until cooked through. Remove and place in a container greased with peanut oil. Roll the pieces of boiled glutinous rice dough until of a springy consistency (illus. 2). Brush the top of each with cooking oil (illus. 3) to prevent them from drying out.

❷ Mix the peanut powder and sugar.

❸ Knead the number of pieces of mochi dough desired and roll in the sweetened peanut powder (illus. 4).

■ These are Hakka style mochi.

菠蘿甜飯

材料：

鳳梨	1個	糖蓮子	$\frac{1}{2}$杯
糯米	1杯	花生油	$\frac{1}{4}$杯
細糖	$\frac{1}{2}$杯	桂圓肉	37公克

❶鳳梨取底段，約8分高(圖1)，挖空果肉，並留下
鳳梨頭當蓋子(圖2)備用。

❷糯米洗淨，用 $\frac{3}{4}$ 杯水蒸熟。

❸桂圓泡水洗淨後撈起。

❹將糯米飯拌入糖、花生油、桂圓肉及糖蓮子，再塞
入鳳梨孔中(圖3)，入蒸鍋大火蒸40分鐘取出，蓋
上鳳梨蓋即可。

Pineapple Rice

INGREDIENTS:

1	whole pineapple
1 c.	glutinous (mochi) rice
37g (1⅓ oz.)	dried longans
½ c.	candied lotus seeds
½ c.	sugar
¼ c.	peanut oil

❶ Cut the pineapple in two at a point about ⁴/₅
of the way from the bottom (illus. 1) and hollow
out the fruit. Retain the rest of the pineapple
as the cover (illus. 2).

❷ Wash the glutinous rice. Add ¾ cup water and
steam until done.

❸ Wash the dried longans, then soak until soft.
Remove from the water.

❹ Stir the sugar, peanut oil, dried longans, and
candied lotus seeds into the glutinous rice.
Stuff in the hollowed out portion of pineapple
(illus. 3). Place in a steamer and steam over
high heat for 40 minutes. Remove from the
steamer, and top with the pineapple "cover."

1　香酥蝦捲：作法見第94頁　Shrimp Rolls (P.94)
2　麵包麻糬：作法見第94頁　Bread Mochi (P.94)
3　紫菜炸雞捲：作法見第95頁　Seaweed Chicken Roll-Ups (P.95)

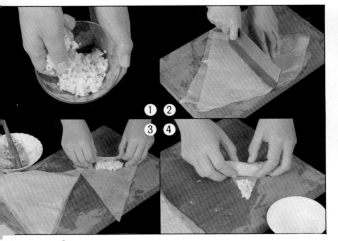

香酥蝦捲

材料 :

①	蝦仁 ……… 225公克		蛋白 ……………… 1個	
	肥猪油 ……… 75公克	②	太白粉 ……… 1大匙	
	香菜葉 ……… 4朶		香油 ……… 1大匙	
荸薺 ……… 4粒			鹽、味精 ‥各 $\frac{1}{2}$ 小匙	
豆腐皮 ……… 4張			胡椒粉、酒…各少許	

❶材料①一起剁碎,荸薺剁碎後擠去水分(圖1)再和②一起加入蝦泥中拌匀。

❷豆腐皮一切爲4張後(圖2),各包入1大匙蝦餡(圖3),再用麵糊粘牢(圖4),入6分熱(約120℃,250°F)油鍋炸至金黃色即可。

■麵糊是以2大匙麵粉加1大匙水拌匀而成。

Shrimp Rolls

INGREDIENTS:

	225g (½ lb.)	shrimp, deveined and shelled
①	75g (2⅔ oz.)	fat pork
	4 leaves	fresh coriander
4		water chestnuts
4 sheets		bean curd skin
	1	egg white
	1 T.	cornstarch
②	1 T.	sesame oil
	½ t.	salt
	dash each:	white pepper, rice wine

❶ Mince ① finely. Mince the water chestnuts and squeeze out excess moisture (illus. 1). Mix the minced water chestnuts and ① into the shrimp-pork paste.

❷ Cut each sheet of bean curd skin into 4 pieces (illus. 2). Wrap one tablespoon of filling in each (illus. 3) and seal with a flour-water paste (illus. 4). Deep-fry in cooking oil heated to 120°C (250°F) until golden.

■ Mix two tablespoons flour with one tablespoon water to make the flour-water paste.

麵包糯糬

材料 :

吐司半條(不切)		水…………… $\frac{1}{2}$ 杯	
鷄 蛋 ……… 4個	①	花生粉 ……… 1杯	
太白粉 ……… 2杯		糖 ……… $\frac{1}{2}$ 杯	

❶吐司去邊後,切成3公分立方塊(圖1)。

❷鷄蛋加半杯水打散。

❸將麵包粒丟入蛋液中泡軟(圖2),撈起後略擠出蛋汁,再滾上太白粉(圖3)。

❹油鍋燒至7分熱(約140℃,280°F),入麵包粒炸成金黃色撈起,再沾上①料即可(圖4)。

Bread Mochi

INGREDIENTS:

half loaf		white bread (uncut)
4		eggs
2 c.		cornstarch
½ c.		water
①	1 c.	peanut powder
	1/2 c.	sugar

❶ Trim the crusts off the bread and cut into 3cm (1¼″) cubes (illus. 1).

❷ Add ½ cup water to the eggs and beat.

❸ Add the bread cubes to the egg mixture, and allow to soak until soft (illus. 2). Remove the bread cubes and lightly squeeze out some of the excess egg mixture. Roll the cubes in cornstarch (illus. 3).

❹ Deep-fry the bread cubes in cooking oil heated to about 140°C (280°F) until golden. Remove from the oil and roll in ① (illus. 4).

紫菜炸雞捲

Seaweed Chicken Roll-Ups

材料：

鶏胸肉	……………	200公克
荸薺	……………	6粒
肥猪油	……………	70公克
薑末	……………	1大匙
紫菜	……………	5張
白芝蔴	……………	$\frac{1}{2}$杯

①
香油	……………	2大匙
太白粉	……………	2大匙
鹽	……………	$\frac{1}{2}$小匙
味精	……………	$\frac{1}{4}$小匙
鮮味露	……………	數滴
胡椒粉	……………	少許

❶鶏胸肉、肥猪油一起剁碎成鶏泥（圖1）。

❷荸薺剁碎後，擠乾水分，與薑末、①一起入鶏泥中拌匀。

❸紫菜剪成4公分寬條狀（圖2），放入1大匙鶏肉泥捲起（圖3），用少許麵糊粘緊，兩端沾上白芝蔴（圖4），入7分熱（約140℃，280°F）油鍋炸熟即可。

■麵糊是以2大匙麵粉加1大匙水拌匀而成。

INGREDIENTS:

200g (7 oz.)	chicken breast fillet
6	water chestnuts
70g (2½ oz.)	fat pork
1 T.	ginger root, minced
5 sheets	purple laver seaweed
½ c.	white sesame seeds, toasted

①
2 T.	sesame oil
2 T.	cornstarch
½ t.	salt
few drops	Maggi sauce
pinch	white pepper

❶ Mince the chicken breast fillet and fat pork together finely to form a paste (illus. 1).

❷ Mince the water chestnuts and squeeze out the excess moisture. Mix thoroughly into the chicken-pork paste together with the minced ginger root and ① .

❸ Cut the purple laver into 4cm (1½″) wide strips (illus. 2). Place one tablespoon chicken-pork filling on each strip of purple laver and roll up (illus. 3). Seal with a little flour-water paste, then dip the two ends in the sesame seeds (illus. 4). Deep-fry in cooking oil heated to about 140°C (280°F) until golden.

■Mix two **tablespoons** flour with one tablespoon water to make the flour-water paste.

八寶腐衣捲

材料：

瘦肉	75公克	豆腐皮	4張
① 芋頭丁	$\frac{1}{2}$ 杯	② 太白粉水	2大匙
竹筍丁	$\frac{1}{2}$ 杯	香油	2大匙
魷魚丁	$\frac{1}{2}$ 杯	醬油	1小匙
蝦米	$\frac{1}{4}$ 杯	糖	$\frac{1}{2}$ 小匙
香菇丁	$\frac{1}{4}$ 杯	味精	$\frac{1}{4}$ 小匙
紅蘿蔔丁	$\frac{1}{4}$ 杯	鹽	$\frac{1}{4}$ 小匙
洋火腿丁	$\frac{1}{4}$ 杯	胡椒粉	少許
沙拉油	1大匙		

❶瘦肉切成小丁，用沙拉油將瘦肉丁及加①料下鍋炒香（圖1），再加②料調味。

❷每張豆腐皮切成4張（圖2），各包入1$\frac{1}{2}$大匙內餡（圖3），捲成春捲狀，用麵粉加水調成糊狀粘緊（圖4），入6分熱 約120℃(250°F)油鍋炸至金黃色即可。

Eight Treasure Bean Curd Rolls

INGREDIENTS:

75g (2⅔ oz.)		lean pork
①	½ c.	taro, pared and diced
	½ c.	bamboo shoots, diced
	½ c.	squid, diced
	¼ c.	dried shrimps
	¼ c.	dried Chinese black mushrooms, soaked until soft and diced
	¼ c.	carrot, diced
	¼ c.	ham, diced
4 sheets		bean curd skin
②	2 T.	cornstarch dissolved in water
	2 T.	sesame oil
	1 t.	soy sauce
	½ t.	sugar
	¼ t.	salt
	pinch	white pepper
1 T.		cooking oil

❶ Dice the lean pork. Stir-fry in the cooking oil with ① until fragrant (illus. 1), then stir in ② to season.

❷ Cut each sheet of bean curd skin into 4 pieces (illus. 2). Fill each piece with 1½ tablespoons filling (illus. 3), then wrap like an eggroll. Seal the bean curd rolls with a flour-and-water paste (illus. 4). Deep-fry in cooking oil heated to about 120°C (250°F) until golden.

蝦仁吐司　　Shrimp Toast

材料：

蝦仁	300公克
肥豬油	75公克
荸薺	6粒
葱白	2根
白芝蔴	3大匙
火腿末	2大匙
吐司	6片

①	蛋白	1個
	太白粉	1大匙
	香油	1大匙
	鹽	$\frac{1}{2}$小匙
	酒	$\frac{1}{2}$小匙
	味精	少許
	胡椒粉	少許

❶蝦仁洗淨後，吸乾水分，再加肥豬油、葱白一起剁成泥狀(圖1)。

❷荸薺剁碎後，擠乾水分(圖2)，再和蝦泥餡拌在一起並加①料調勻。

❸吐司去邊後，塗上$\frac{1}{6}$之蝦泥並抹平(圖3)，再以白芝蔴、火腿末裝飾。

❹油鍋燒至6分熱(約120℃，250°Ｆ)，入蝦仁吐司炸至金黃色，撈起並切成4塊即可(圖4)。

INGREDIENTS:

300g (2/3 lb.)	shrimp, deveined and shelled
75g (2 2/3 oz.)	fat pork
6	water chestnuts
2	green onions, white part only
3 T.	white sesame seeds
2 T.	ham, minced
6 slices	white bread

①	1	egg white
	1 T.	cornstarch
	1 T.	sesame oil
	½ t.	salt
	½ t.	rice wine
	pinch	white pepper

❶ Wash the shrimp, then carefully squeeze dry. Add the fat pork and the green onion whites and mince finely to form a paste (illus. 1).

❷ Mince the water chestnuts, then squeeze out the excess moisture (illus. 2). Add the minced water chestnuts and ① to the shrimp paste and mix thoroughly.

❸ Trim the crusts off the white bread. Spread ⅙ of the shrimp paste on each slice, smoothing over the top of each (illus. 3). Sprinkle some white sesame seed and minced ham over the tops as a garnish.

❹ Heat oil for frying to about 120°C (250°F). Fry the shrimp toast until golden. Remove from the oil and cut each slice into quarters (illus. 4).

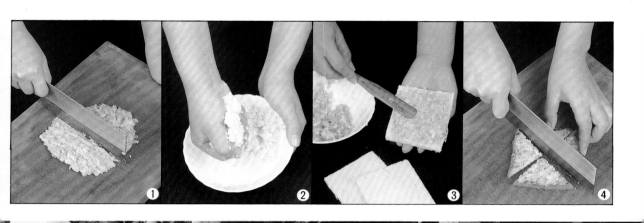

隨意包

As-You-Please Crêpes

材料：
外皮：

水 ……………………………	1½杯
低筋麵粉 …………………	1杯
太白粉 ………………………	¼杯
奶水 …………………………	¼杯
軟凍粉 ……………………	2大匙
蛋 ……………………………	2個
香草片 ……………………	4片

內餡：

洋火腿 ……………………	8片
小黃瓜 ……………………	8片
橫切洋葱 …………………	4片
生菜葉 ……………………	4片
沙拉 …………………………	½杯
沙拉油 ……………………	少許

❶外皮材料揉拌均勻後，放置半小時，再略攪勻（圖1），用抹過油的平底鍋烘煎成4張直徑20公分的薄餅（圖2），煎時用小火並避免焦黃翻面再略烘一下。

❷每張麵皮上置一張生菜葉、洋葱片、2片火腿、小黃瓜，再淋上1大匙沙拉醬（圖3），最後捲成自己喜愛之形狀即可（圖4）。

■內餡可隨自己喜好而改變，或包豆沙類甜餡，或醬肉類鹹餡或冰淇淋類亦可，故名隨意包。

INGREDIENTS:
Wrappers:

1½ c.	water
1 c.	low gluten (cake) flour
¼ c.	cornstarch
¼ c.	evaporated milk
2 T.	custard powder
1 drop	vanilla extract
2	eggs

Filling:

8 slices	ham
8 slices	pickling cucumber
4 slices	onion
4 leaves	lettuce
½ c.	mayonnaise
as needed	cooking oil

❶ Mix the wrapper ingredients and leave undisturbed one half hour. Mix a second time until smooth (illus. 1). Pour ¼ of the batter onto an oiled frying pan or griddle and bake over low heat into a 20cm (8″) diameter crêpe (illus. 2). Do not allow to brown. Turn over to bake on the other side. Repeat 3 more times to use up the batter.

❷ On each crêpe, place a lettuce leaf, a slice of onion, 2 slices of ham, and 2 slices of cucumber. Top with some mayonnaise (illus. 3). Roll up to eat (illus. 4).

■ The filling ingredients can be varied according to personal preference. Try soy-stewed pork or beef, or a sweet filling, such as sweet red bean paste or ice cream.

炸芋頭餃 　　　Taro Balls

材料
外皮：
　去皮芋頭 ……………600公克
　豬油 …………………120公克
　熟澄麵 ………………100公克
　澄粉 …………………100公克
　細糖 …………………1大匙
　鹽 ……………………1小匙
　胡椒粉 ………………½小匙
　胺粉 …………………¼小匙
內餡：
　瘦肉丁 ………………150公克
　香菇丁 ………………40公克
　蝦米 …………………40公克
　葱酥 …………………2大匙
　荸薺末 ………………½杯
①｛
　水 ……………………½杯
　酒 ……………………1小匙
　鹽 ……………………½小匙
　味精 …………………⅛小匙
　胡椒粉、鮮味露 ……各少許
沙拉油 …………………3大匙

❶芋頭切塊蒸熟，並趁熱搗碎（圖1），加入外皮其它
材料，拌勻成芋泥糰（圖2），並分成如乒乓球之大
小塊。

❷瘦肉丁用3大匙油炒熟後，加入內餡其它材料及①
料，炒勻後（圖3），略爲冰凍。

❸每份芋泥包入1大匙內餡後（圖4），入6分熱（約
120℃，250°F）油鍋炸至金黃色即可。

■熟澄麵作法：澄粉加滾水燙熟。

INGREDIENTS:
Dough:
600g (1⅓ lb.)	taros, pared
120g (¼ lb.)	lard or shortening
100g (3½ oz.)	wheat starch mixed into boiling water
100g (3½ oz.)	wheat starch
1 T.	sugar
1 t.	salt
½ t.	white pepper
¼ t.	ammonia bicarbonate

Filling:
150g (⅓ lb.)	lean pork, diced
40g (1½ oz.)	dried Chinese black mushrooms, soaked until soft and diced
40g (1½ oz.)	dried shrimps
2 T.	fried green onion flakes
½ c.	water chestnuts, minced

① ｛
½ c.	water
1 t.	rice wine
½ t.	salt
dash each:	white pepper, Maggi sauce

| 3 T. | cooking oil |

❶ Cut the taros into chunks and steam until soft. Mash until smooth while still hot (illus. 1). Add the remaining dough ingredients and mix well. Make into balls about the size of ping pong balls (illus. 2).

❷ Stir-fry the minced lean pork in 3 table-spoons cooking oil until done. Add the remaining filling ingredients and ① and continue to stir-fry until cooked through (illus. 3). Freeze until partially solid.

❸ Wrap one tablespoon filling in each piece of taro dough (illus. 4). Deep-fry in cooking oil heated to about 120°C (250°F) until golden. Remove and drain.

八寶芋泥

Eight Treasure Taro Paste

材料：

大芋頭	……………………	375公克
①	細糖	……………………	75公克
	豬油	……………………	3大匙
	奶水	……………………	3大匙
	蛋	……………………	1個
	元宵粉	……………………	¼杯

①
- 細糖 …………………… 75公克
- 豬油 …………………… 3大匙
- 奶水 …………………… 3大匙
- 蛋 …………………… 1個
- 元宵粉 …………………… ¼杯

②（圖1）
- 桔餅切碎 …………………… 2大匙
- 冬瓜糖切碎 …………………… 2大匙
- 葡萄干 …………………… 2大匙
- 糖蓮子 …………………… 2大匙
- 桂圓肉 …………………… 2大匙
- 蜜棗肉 …………………… 2大匙
- 蜜餞青李肉 …………………… 2大匙
- 鳳梨乾切碎 …………………… 2大匙

③
- 奶水 …………………… ½杯
- 細糖 …………………… ¼杯
- 水 …………………… ¼杯

太白粉、水 …………………… 各2大匙
沙拉油 …………………… 1小匙

❶芋頭去皮、切塊、蒸熟、趁熱搗碎，加入①料拌勻

❷容器先塗上一層沙拉油，再把②料排列在容器內，接著再塡入芋泥(圖2)。

❸將芋泥入蒸籠，大火蒸40分鐘取出，扣於盤上（圖3）。

❹③料煮開後，加太白粉水芶芡，淋於八寶芋泥上（圖4）即可。

INGREDIENTS:

375g (13 oz.)	large taros	
①	75g (2⅔ oz.)	sugar
	3 T.	lard or shortening
	3 T.	evaporated milk
	1	egg
	¼ c.	glutinous rice (mochi) flour
②	2 T.	candied kumquats, minced
	2 T.	wintermelon candy, minced
	2 T.	raisins
	2 T.	candied lotus seeds
	2 T.	dried longans
	2 T.	seedless preserved Chinese dates (or prunes)
	2 T.	preserved Chinese plums
	2 T.	dried pineapple, minced
③	½ c.	evaporated milk
	¼ c.	sugar
	¼ c.	water
2 T. each:	cornstarch, water	
1 t.	cooking oil	

❶ Pare the taros, cut into chunks, and steam until soft. Mash into a smooth paste while hot. Mix in ①

❷ Oil a steaming bowl. Arrange the ingredients in ② in the bowl, then spread the taro paste over the top (illus. 2).

❸ Place the bowl in a steamer and steam 40 minutes over high heat. Remove from the steamer and invert onto a plate (illus. 3).

❹ Bring ③ to a boil, thicken with the cornstarch, and drizzle over the taro paste (illus. 4).

荸薺餅

Water Chestnut-Date Balls

材料：

荸薺	……………………	600公克
太白粉	……………………	2大匙
棗泥	……………………	120公克
太白粉、水	…………………	各1大匙
熟白芝蔴	……………………	2大匙
① { 細糖	……………………	4大匙
桂花醬	……………………	¼小匙
水	……………………	2杯

❶荸薺剁成細末後，略擠乾水分（圖1），再加入太白粉拌勻。

❷棗泥分成12等份，每份再裹上荸薺末，使成為如乒乓球狀（圖2）。

❸炸油熱至130℃（270°F），放入荸薺餅，炸成金黃色撈起。

❹另鍋中入水2杯，加①料及荸薺餅用中火煮5分鐘，再取起荸薺餅置於盤裡，並略為壓扁（圖3）。

❺鍋中所剩之餅湯汁，用太白粉水芶茨後，淋於荸薺餅上（圖4），並灑上芝蔴即可。

INGREDIENTS:

600g (1⅓ lb.)	water chestnuts
2 T.	cornstarch
120g (¼ lb.)	Chinese date paste
1 T. each:	cornstarch, water
2 T.	white sesame seeds, toasted
① { 4 T.	sugar
¼ t.	sweet osmanthus jam
2 c.	water

❶ Mince the water chestnuts. Squeeze out the excess moisture (illus.1) and mix with the cornstarch.

❷ Divide the Chinese date paste into 12 equally sized portions. Roll each portion of date paste in the minced water chestnuts to the size of a ping pong ball (illus. 2).

❸ Heat oil for frying to 130°C (270°F). Deep-fry the water chestnut-date balls until golden and remove from the oil.

❹ Add 2 cups water to a saucepan or wok. Add ① and the water chestnut-date balls, and cook over medium heat for 5 minutes. Remove the balls to a plate and allow to cool. Flatten the balls lightly (illus. 3).

❺ Thicken the liquid remaining from step ❹ with cornstarch and drizzle over the water chestnut-date balls (illus. 4). Sprinkle the sesame seeds over the top.

蝦仁雲吞　Shrimp Wontons

材料：

材料	份量
蝦仁	200公克
餛飩皮	24張
芹菜末	2大匙

①
蛋白	半個
太白粉	1大匙
香油	1小匙
鹽	$\frac{1}{4}$小匙
味精	$\frac{1}{8}$小匙

②
雞湯	6杯
鹽	1小匙
味精	$\frac{1}{4}$小匙
胡椒粉、酒	各少許
芹菜末	少許
香油	數滴
鮮味露	數滴

❶蝦仁洗淨，吸乾水份（圖1），略爲切碎，再與芹菜末、①料拌勻甩打（圖2）。

❷每張餛飩皮包入1小匙內餡。

❸②料先煮開盛碗，將5杯水煮開，放入餛飩，煮至浮起（圖3），加入半杯冷水煮開後續煮1分鐘，撈起盛入湯碗中即可。

INGREDIENTS:

200g (7 oz.)		shrimp, shelled
2 T.		Chinese celery, minced
24		wonton wrappers

①
½	egg white
1 T.	cornstarch
1 t.	sesame oil
¼ t.	salt

②
6 c.	chicken stock
1 t.	salt
dash each:	white pepper, rice wine
few drops	sesame oil
as desired	minced Chinese celery
few drops	Maggi sauce

❶ Wash the shrimp, squeeze out the excess moisture (illus. 1), and chop coarsely. Mix with ① and the minced Chinese celery and fling against a cutting board or counter several times to increase elasticity (illus. 2).

❷ Wrap one teablespoon filling in each wonton wrapper.

❸ Bring ② to a boil and pour into a soup bowl. Bring 5 cups water to a boil and drop in the wontons. Cook until the wontons rise to the top (illus. 3). Add a half cup cold water and continue to cook another minute. Remove the wontons from the water and place in the prepared chicken broth.

1

2

3

脆皮蠔捲

Fresh Oyster Rolls

材料：

鮮蠔 ……………300公克	香油 …………2大匙
絞肉 ……………225公克	醬油 …………2小匙
韭黃 ……………150公克	① 酒 …………1小匙
葱花……………½杯	鹽 …………½小匙
春捲皮……………15張	味精 …………¼小匙
	胡椒粉…………少許
	太白粉、水 ……各2大匙

❶鮮蠔入鍋川燙（圖1），去腥味，韭黃切末均備用。

❷絞肉入鍋炒熟後，加葱花及①料拌匀，再加鮮蠔及韭黃拌匀，並用太白粉、水芶芡成內餡（圖2）。

❸春捲皮攤開，包入1大匙內餡，捲起後用麵糊粘牢（圖3），再入7分熱（約140℃，280°F）油鍋炸至金黃色即可。

■麵糊是以2大匙麵粉加1大匙水拌匀而成。

INGREDIENTS:

300g (⅔ lb.)		fresh oysters
225g (½ lb.)		ground pork
150g (⅓ lb.)		yellow Chinese chives
½ c.		chopped green onion
15		spring roll wrappers
①	2 t.	sesame oil
	2 t.	soy sauce
	1 t.	rice wine
	½ t.	salt
	pinch	white pepper
2 T. each:		cornstarch, water

❶ Blanch the fresh oysters briefly in boiling water (illus. 1) to get rid of any fishy taste. Mince the yellow Chinese chives.

❷ Stir-fry the ground pork until cooked through. Add the chopped green onion and ① , mixing well. Add the oysters and minced yellow Chinese chives. Thicken with the cornstarch dissolved in water to form the filling (illus. 2).

❸ Wrap one tablespoon filling in each spring roll wrapper. Roll and seal with some flour-water paste (illus. 3). Deep-fry in cooking oil heated to 140°C (280°F) until golden.

■ Mix two tablespoons flour with one tablespoon water to make the flour-water paste.

脆皮豆腐捲

材料：

豆腐	·······2塊		蛋白	·······1個
① 髮菜	·······½杯	②	太白粉	·······2大匙
熟青豆	·······¼杯		香油	·······1大匙
熟紅蘿蔔丁	·······¼杯		鹽	·······½小匙
豆腐皮	·······4張		胡椒粉、味精	·······各少許
麵糊	·······¼杯			

❶豆腐去表皮後，略搗碎，用細紗布擠乾水分（圖4），和①、②料拌勻。

❷每張豆腐皮切成4小張，每小張包入1大匙豆腐餡（圖5），捲起後用麵糊粘牢（圖6），入6分熱（約120℃，250℉）油鍋炸至金黃色即可。

Bean Curd Rolls

INGREDIENTS:

2 cakes		bean curd
	½ c.	hair seaweed (fa-ts'ai)
①	¼ c.	peas, cooked
	¼ c.	carrots, cooked and diced
4 sheets		bean curd skin
¼ c.		flour-water paste
	1	egg white
	2 T.	cornstarch
②	1 T.	sesame oil
	½ t.	salt
	pinch	white pepper

❶ Trim off the tough edges of the bean curd, then mash coarsely. Place the mashed bean curd in some fine-mesh gauze and squeeze out the excess moisture (illus. 4). Mix ① and ② into the mashed bean curd until well blended.

❷ Cut each sheet of bean curd skin into 4 pieces. Wrap one tablespoon of the bean curd filling in each and roll as shown (illus. 5). Seal with a flour-and-water paste (illus. 6). Deep-fry in cooking oil heated to about 120°C (250°F) until golden.

銀蘿軟絲捲

Radish Roulades

材料：

花枝	300公克
肥豬油	75公克
香菜末	$\frac{1}{3}$ 杯
白蘿蔔	1條
紫菜	1張
鹽	2大匙

① {
蛋白	1個
太白粉	2大匙
香油	1大匙
鹽	$\frac{1}{2}$ 小匙
味精	$\frac{1}{4}$ 小匙
胡椒粉、酒	各少許

❶花枝加肥豬油剁碎後，加入香菜末與①料拌勻。

❷白蘿蔔切0.2×4×10公分之薄片，先用2大匙鹽醃軟後洗淨，擦乾水分（圖1）。

❸紫菜剪成1×8公分長條狀。

❹每片白蘿蔔，包入1大匙內餡（圖2），再用紫菜在腰段處捲起（圖3），入蒸鍋大火蒸8分鐘即可。

INGREDIENTS:

300g (²/₃ lb.)	squid, cleaned
75g (2²/₃ oz.)	fat pork
¹/₃ c.	fresh coriander, minced
1	Chinese white radish (daikon)
1 sheet	purple laver seaweed
2 T.	salt

① {
1	egg white
2 T.	cornstarch
1 T.	sesame oil
½ t.	salt
dash each:	white pepper, rice wine

❶ Mince the squid together with the fat pork. Mix in the minced fresh coriander and ① .

❷ Cut the Chinese white radish into 0.2 x 4 x 10cm ($^1/_{12}$″ x $1^1/_2$″ x 4″) thin slices. Mix in 2 tablespoons salt and allow to set until soft. Rinse off the salt and pat dry (illus. 1).

❸ Cut the purple laver into 1 x 8cm (½″ x 3¼″) strips.

❹ Roll up one tablespoon meat filling in each strip of Chinese white radish (illus. 2), then wrap with a strip of purple laver as shown (illus. 3). Arrange in a steamer and steam over high heat for 8 minutes.

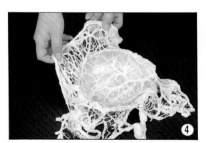

網油燒白

材料：

糯米 …………………1杯	①	葡萄乾、碎桔餅、糖蓮子…各 $\frac{1}{4}$ 杯
豆沙…………………75公克		細糖、花生油………………各 $\frac{1}{4}$ 杯
豬網油 ………………1張		花生粉……………………… $\frac{1}{3}$ 杯

❶糯米洗淨後，加1杯水蒸熟，並拌入①料。

❷網油洗淨後，舖於碗底（圖4）。

❸豆沙壓扁成直徑8公分之圓形，置於糯米飯中間，再把飯糰填入碗裡，將多出之網油翻起蓋住米飯（圖5）。

❹將米飯入蒸鍋，大火蒸40分鐘後取出，扣於盤裡（圖6），邊緣再灑上花生粉即可。

Red Bean Fruit Rice

INGREDIENTS:

1 c.		glutinous (mochi) rice
75g (2⅔ oz.)		sweet red bean paste
1 piece		net lard
①	¼ c.	raisins
	¼ c.	candied kumquats, minced
	¼ c.	candied lotus seeds
	¼ c.	sugar
	¼ c.	peanut oil
⅓ c.		peanut powder

❶ Wash the glutinous rice, then add 1 cup water and steam until cooked through. Mix in the ingredients in ① .

❷ Wash the net lard thoroughly and spread over the bottom of a steaming bowl (illus. 4).

❸ Press the sweet red bean paste into an 8cm (3″) circle and wrap inside the glutinous rice. Place the filled glutinous rice in the net lard-lined bowl. Cover the rice with the overhanging portion of the net lard (illus. 5)

❹ Place the red bean fruit rice in a steamer and steam over high heat for 40 minutes. Remove and invert onto a serving plate (illus.6). Sprinkle some peanut powder around the edge.

椰蓉西米露

材料：

芋頭	300公克
細糖	200公克
西谷米	150公克
椰子粉	50公克
煉乳	$\frac{1}{2}$ 杯
水	14杯

❶芋頭去皮洗淨切塊蒸熟，再加4杯水打成糊狀（圖1）。

❷將芋糊倒入鍋中，再加煉乳、砂糖和4杯水，用中火煮開後，續入椰子粉拌勻起鍋（圖2）。

❸另鍋中6杯水，煮開，放入西谷米用小火煮至透明（圖3）後，撈起，放入芋頭汁中拌勻即可。

Sago in Coconut Milk

INGREDIENTS:

300g (²⁄₃ lb.)	taro
200g (9½ oz.)	sugar
150g (⅓ lb.)	pearl sago or tapioca
50g (1¾ oz.)	desiccated coconut
½ c.	sweetened condensed milk
14 c.	water

❶ Wash and pare the taros. Cut in chunks and steam until soft. Puree in a blender with 4 cups water (illus. 1).

❷ Pour the puree in a saucepan, then add the sweetened condensed milk, sugar, and 4 cups water. Bring to a boil over medium heat, then add the desiccated coconut. Stir until well blended and pour into a bowl (illus. 2).

❸ In another saucepan, bring 6 cups of water to a boil. Add the pearl sago or tapioca and cook over low heat until transparent (illus. 3). Drain the pearl sago or tapioca, add to the taro coconut mixture, and stir well.

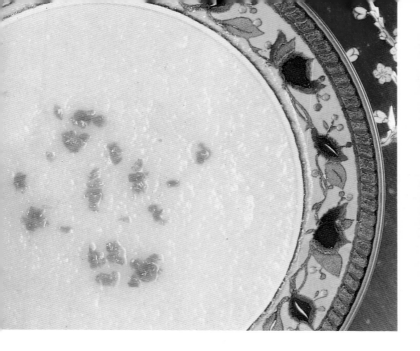

蘋果甜糊

材料：

蘋果 ································4個
細糖 ·····························$\frac{3}{4}$杯
水 ································5杯

① {
元宵粉 ·····················$\frac{1}{2}$杯
水 ··························$\frac{3}{4}$杯
}

❶蘋果去皮、籽後，切成塊狀，放入蒸鍋中大火蒸10分鐘取出（圖4），加水打成汁。

❷蘋果汁加糖用中火煮開（圖5），再用①料芶芡倒入碗中即可（圖6）。

Chinese Applesauce

INGREDIENTS:

4	apples
¾ c.	sugar
5 c.	water
① { ½ c. / ¾ c. }	glutinous rice (mochi) flour / water

❶ Pare and slice the apples, removing seeds. Steam for 10 minutes over high heat (illus. 4). Add the water and liquefy in a blender.

❷ Add the sugar to the apple juice and bring to a boil over medium heat (illus. 5). Thicken with ① and pour in a bowl (illus. 6).

炸棗泥香蕉捲

材料：

棗泥	150公克	①	中筋麵粉	1杯
大香蕉	4條		太白粉	¼杯
			軟凍粉	2大匙

❶香蕉去皮後切成4公分長段，再將中間挖空（圖1），用棗泥填滿（圖2）。

❷①料加1杯水調成麵糊。

❸香蕉捲裹上麵糊後（圖3），入7分熱（約140℃，280°F）油鍋炸至金黃色即可。

Stuffed Bananas

INGREDIENTS:

150g (⅓ lb.)	Chinese date paste
4	large bananas
①	1 c.	all-purpose (medium gluten) flour
	¼ c.	cornstarch
	2 T.	custard powder

❶ Peel the bananas, cut into 4cm (1½″) sections, and hollow out the centers (illus. 1). Fill with the Chinese date paste (illus. 2).

❷ Add one cup water to ① to make a batter.

❸ Dip the stuffed bananas in the batter (illus. 3) and deep-fry in cooking oil heated to 140°C (280°F) until golden.

椰蓉豆沙鍋餅

材料：

①	水	¾杯	內餡：	
	中筋麵粉	75公克	豆沙	150公克
	鷄蛋	1個	椰子粉	¼杯
	熟白芝蔴	2大匙		
	香草片	3片		

❶將①材料拌均勻成麵糊，再煎成一張大薄餅（圖4）。

❷豆沙餡提成12×18公分之長方形後放在大薄餅上，再灑上椰子粉（圖5）。

❸薄餅將豆沙包捲起來（圖6），用小火煎至兩面金黃，取出切成12小塊即可。

Coconut-Red Bean Pot Stickers

INGREDIENTS:
Batter:

①	¾ c.	water
	75g (2⅔ oz.)	all-purpose (medium gluten) flour
	1	egg
	2 T.	white sesame seeds, toasted
	1 drop	vanilla extract

Filling:

| 150g (⅓ lb.) | sweet red bean paste |
| ¼ c. | desiccated (or flaked) coconut |

❶ Mix ① and fry into a pancake (illus. 4).

❷ Roll the bean paste to 12×18cm (5″×7¼″). Place on the pancake and sprinkle on the coconut (illus. 5).

❸ Roll the pancake (illus. 6) and fry over low heat until golden. Cut into 12 pieces.

芝蔴鍋炸

材料：

①	水	3杯
	中筋麵粉	2杯
	奶水	½杯
	鷄蛋	5個
	細糖	150公克
	香草片	5片

	太白粉	1½杯
②	熟白芝蔴粉	1杯
	細糖	½杯

❶ 1 料混合均勻後，放入鍋中用小火煮開成糊狀，再倒入塗過油的托盤裡（圖7）、待涼、放入冰箱冷凍2小時。

❷ 取出凝固之鍋炸，切成所要之塊狀（圖8），沾上乾太白粉（圖9）後，入7分熱（約140℃，280°F）油鍋炸至金黃色撈起，再沾上混勻之2料，並趁熱供食。

Sesame Crisps

INGREDIENTS:

①	3 c.	water
	2 c.	all-purpose (medium gluten) flour
	½ c.	evaporated milk
	5	eggs
	150g (⅓ lb.)	sugar
	⅛ t.	vanilla extract
	1½ c.	cornstarch
②	1 c.	white sesame seeds, toasted and ground into a powder
	½ c.	sugar

❶ Mix ① until smooth. Thicken in a saucepan over low heat until the consistency of pancake batter. Pour into an oiled cake pan (illus. 7). Allow to cool, then refrigerate for 2 hours.

❷ Cut the cooled batter into the desired size pieces (illus. 8), then dredge in dry cornstarch (illus. 9). Deep-fry in cooking oil heated to about 140°C (280°F) until golden. Remove from oil and dip in ② . Serve hot.

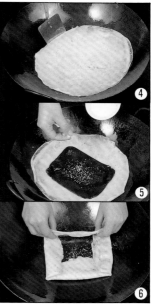

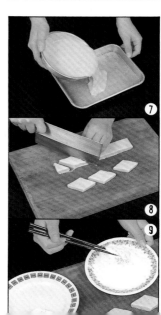

什錦海鮮粥

材料：

白飯	……1碗	油條	……1條
蛤蜊	……4個	香菜	……¼杯
鮮魷魚	……1小條	大蒜酥	……2大匙
沙蝦	……6隻	①{ 鹽	……1小匙
靑蟹	……1隻	胡椒粉	……¼小匙
生蠔、鱈魚肉‥各75公克		味精	……¼小匙

❶海鮮材料切好，入開水川燙備用。

❷白飯加6杯水煮軟，放入海鮮和大蒜酥煮透（圖1），並加①料調味。

❸油條切碎置碗中（圖2），將煮好的海產粥倒入碗裡和油條拌勻（圖3），再灑上香菜即可。

Seafood Congee

INGREDIENTS:

1 rice bowl	cooked white rice
4	fresh clams
1 each:	small fresh squid, crab
75g (2⅔ oz.) each:	fresh oysters, cod fillet
6	shrimp
1	Chinese fried cruller (yu-t'iao)
2 T.	fried garlic flakes
¼ c.	fresh coriander
6 c.	water
① { 1 t.	salt
¼ t.	white pepper

❶ Cut the squid, cod, and crab. Blanch all the seafood in boiling water.

❷ Add 6 cups water to the cooked white rice and boil until soft. Add the seafood and the fried garlic flakes and cook until done (illus. 1). Stir in ① to season.

❸ Cut the Chinese fried cruller in small pieces and place in a bowl (illus. 2). Pour the seafood congee in the bowl, stir (illus. 3), then sprinkle some fresh coriander over the top.

皮蛋瘦肉粥

材料：

白飯	……1碗	①{ 鹽	……1小匙
皮蛋	……2個	香油	……1小匙
鷄湯	……4杯	味精	……¼小匙
玉米醬	……1杯	胡椒粉	……少許
瘦猪肉	……112公克	葱花、油	……各2大匙

❶皮蛋煮熟，去殼後切小丁（圖4），猪肉剁碎。

❷油2大匙，先炒熟猪肉，入鷄湯和白飯煮軟（圖5），再入皮蛋、玉米醬及①料，煮稠後起鍋（圖6），灑入葱花即可。

Pork Congee with 1,000-Year-Old Egg

INGREDIENTS:

2	1,000-year-old preserved eggs
112g (¼ lb.)	lean pork
1 c.	cream style corn
1 rice bowl	cooked white rice
4 c.	chicken stock
① { 1 t.	salt
1 t.	sesame oil
pinch	pepper
2 T.	chopped green onion
2 T.	cooking oil

❶ Cook the preserved eggs, shell, and dice (illus. 4). Mince the pork.

❷ Stir-fry the pork in 2 tablespoons cooking oil until done. Add the chicken stock and cooked white rice and cook until soft (illus. 5). Add the preserved egg, cream style corn, and 1. Cook until thick (illus. 6). Pour into a serving bowl and top with chopped green onion.

冬菇鷄球粥

材料：

白飯	…………………………1碗	
油條	…………………………半條	
鷄胸肉	………………………120公克	
香菇	…………………………20公克	
鷄湯	…………………………4杯	

① { 鹽 …………………………1小匙
味精 ………………………¼小匙
胡椒粉 ……………………少許
香菜 ………………………2大匙

❶ 鷄胸肉去皮、骨（圖7），剁成約1公分立方小塊，香菇亦切成小塊，油條切碎放置碗裡。

❷ 鷄肉、香菇先用開水煮過，以去腥味。

❸ 白飯、鷄湯先下鍋煮軟，再放入鷄肉、香菇及①料煮透（圖8），最後用中火熬煮至稠狀，倒入碗裡（圖9）灑上香菜即可。

Chicken-Mushroom Congee

INGREDIENTS:

120g (¼ lb.)	chicken breast fillet
20g (⅔ oz.)	dried Chinese black mushrooms
half	Chinese fried cruller (yu-t'iao)
1 rice bowl	cooked white rice
4 c.	chicken stock
① { 1 t.	salt
pinch	white pepper
2 T.	fresh coriander

❶ Remove the skin and bone from the chicken breast if not using prepared fillets (illus. 7). Dice into 1cm (⅜") cubes. Soak the dried Chinese black mushrooms until soft and dice. Crush the Chinese fried cruller and put in a bowl.

❷ Parboil the chicken and mushrooms. Drain.

❸ Boil the cooked rice in the chicken stock until soft. Add the chicken, mushrooms and ① and boil until cooked through (illus. 8). Continue to cook over medium heat until the congee has thickened. Pour into the bowl with the Chinese fried crullers (illus. 9) and top with chopped fresh coriander.

三鮮鍋餅

材料：
外皮：
　蛋 ……………………1個
　水 ………………150公克
　中筋麵粉 ………75公克 ①
　太白粉 …………37公克
內餡：
　絞肉 …………112公克
　蝦仁 ……………75公克
　干貝（泡軟）……2大匙

香油 …………1大匙
太白粉 ………1大匙
蠔油 …………1小匙 ①
鹽 ……………½小匙
味精 …………少許
酒、胡椒粉、鮮味露
　………………各少許
沙拉油 …………2小匙

❶外皮材料打勻成麵糊。
❷內餡材料加①料調勻後備用。
❸將鍋燒熱後，均勻地擦上一層油（保持不流動狀態），倒入麵糊後，攤成圓形，（圖1）並用小火烘乾。
❹將內餡亦攤於圓形麵皮上（圖2），將多餘麵皮摺起包住內餡（圖3），再用小火煎至兩面呈金黃即可。

Pork-Seafood Crêpe

INGREDIENTS:
Wrapper:

1	egg
150g (⅓ lb.)	water
75g (2⅔ oz.)	all-purpose (medium gluten) flour
37g (1⅓ oz.)	cornstarch

Filling:

112g (¼ lb.)	ground pork
75g (2⅔ oz.)	shrimp, shelled
2 T.	dried scallops, soaked until soft and shredded

①	1 T.	sesame oil
	1 T.	cornstarch
	1 t.	oyster sauce
	½ t.	salt
	dash each:	rice wine, white pepper, Maggi sauce

❶ Mix the wrapper ingredients into a batter.
❷ Mix the filling ingredients and ① until well combined.
❸ Heat a flat frying pan or wok and brush on a layer of cooking oil. (There should not be so much oil that it can move around the pan.) Pour the batter into the frying pan, spreading it evenly over the bottom into a round shape (illus. 1), and fry over low heat until dry.
❹ Spread the meat filling into a round shape on the flour wrapper (illus. 2). Fold up the edges of the wrapper to wrap up the filling (illus. 3). Continue to fry on both sides over low heat until golden.

珍珠丸子　　Pearl Balls

材料：

長糯米	……………………… 1杯
洋火腿末	……………………… $\frac{1}{4}$杯

① ｛ 絞後腿肉 ……………300公克
　　 荸薺末 …………………4粒

香油 ……………………… 2大匙

② ｛ 太白粉 ……………………1大匙
　　 醬油 ……………………1大匙
　　 鹽 ……………………… $\frac{1}{2}$小匙
　　 胡椒粉、酒、味精 ……各少許

香菜葉 ………………………37公克

❶長糯米洗淨後，泡水4小時，瀝乾，再與火腿末拌勻備用。

❷①、②料拌勻用打數下後，擠成如乒乓球大小之肉丸(圖1)，再沾裹糯米(圖2)，入蒸籠，大火蒸8分鐘，取出上飾香菜葉(圖3)即可。

Pearl Balls

INGREDIENTS:

1 c.	long-grained glutinous rice
¼ c.	minced ham
① ｛ 300g (⅔ lb.)	ground pork (hind leg meat)
4	water chestnuts, minced
37g (1⅓ oz.)	fresh coriander leaves
② ｛ 2 T.	sesame oil
1 T.	cornstarch
1 T.	soy sauce
½ t.	salt
dash each:	white pepper, rice wine

❶ Wash the glutinous rice and soak in water to more than cover for 4 hours. Drain and mix in the minced ham.

❷ Mix ① and ② until well blended. Fling against a cutting board or counter several times to increase elasticity. Form into balls about the size of ping pong balls (illus. 1). Roll in the soaked glutinous rice and ham mixture (illus. 2). Arrange in a steamer and steam over high heat for 8 minutes. Remove from steamer and garnish with the coriander leaves (illus. 3).

潤餅捲

材料：

①	銀芽 …………1杯	②	香油 …………2大匙
	韮黃段 …………1杯		鹽、味精…各 $\frac{1}{2}$ 小匙
	筍絲 …………1杯		胡椒粉 …………少許
	香菇絲 ………… $\frac{1}{3}$ 杯	③	花生粉 ………… $\frac{1}{2}$ 杯
	紅蘿蔔絲 ………… $\frac{1}{3}$ 杯		細糖 ………… $\frac{1}{4}$ 杯

香菜 ………… $\frac{1}{2}$ 杯　　甜辣醬 ………… $\frac{1}{2}$ 杯

潤餅皮 …………12張　　油 …………2大匙

❶ 以2大匙油將①料全部下鍋炒熟後，加②料調味備用。③料亦拌勻備用。

❷ 潤餅皮攤開後，先塗上1小匙甜辣醬（圖1），再灑上1小匙花生粉，而後再放入2大匙菜餡（圖2），最上面再加少許香菜後，捲起如春捲狀（圖3）即可

Lumpia

INGREDIENTS:

①	1 c.	bean sprouts, both ends removed
	1 c.	yellow Chinese chives, cut in 2½" lengths
	1 c.	bamboo shoots, julienned
	⅓ c.	dried Chinese black mushrooms, soaked until soft and julienned
	⅓ c.	carrots, julienned
	½ c.	fresh coriander
	12	lumpia wrappers (Shanghai spring roll wrappers; thinner than Cantonese style)
②	2 T.	sesame oil
	½ t.	salt
	pinch	white pepper
③	½ c.	peanut powder
	¼ c.	sugar
	½ c.	Taiwanese sweet hot sauce
	2 T.	cooking oil

❶ Preheat a wok and add two tablespoons cooking oil. Stir-fry the ingredients in ① until cooked through. Stir in ② to season. Remove from heat. Mix the ingredients in ③ until well blended.

❷ Open up a lumpia wrapper. Brush on 1 tea - spoon of Taiwanese sweet hot sauce (illus. 1), then sprinkle on 1 teaspoon of peanut powder. Add 2 tablespoons of the vegetable filling (illus. 2), and top with a little fresh coriander. Wrap like an eggroll (illus. 3).

❶

❷

❸

牛肉丸子

材料：

牛里肌肉	⋯⋯600公克	葱花	⋯⋯½杯
① 水	⋯⋯375公克	香菜葉	⋯⋯½杯
肥猪油	⋯⋯150公克	蠔油	⋯⋯2大匙
陳皮（圖1）	⋯18公克	香油	⋯⋯2大匙
蘇打粉（圖1）	⋯1小匙	② 糖	⋯⋯4小匙
蛋白	⋯⋯2個	鹽	⋯⋯½小匙
		味精	⋯⋯¼小匙
		太白粉	⋯⋯75公克
		馬蹄粉（圖1）	
			⋯⋯37公克

❶牛里肌肉剁碎，加入①料拌醃1小時備用。

❷將醃過之牛肉，加入②料拌勻，蛋白打發（圖2），亦加入拌勻備用。

❸擠成如乒乓球大小之肉丸（圖3），入蒸籠大火蒸8分鐘即可。

Steamed Beef Balls

INGREDIENTS:

	600g (1⅓ lb.)	lean beef
①	375g (13 oz.)	water
	150g (⅓ lb.)	fat pork
	18g (⅔ oz.)	dried tangerine peel (illus. 1)
	1 t.	baking soda (illus. 1)
2		egg whites
	2 T.	oyster sauce
	2 T.	sesame oil
	4 t.	sugar
	½ t.	salt
②	75g (2½ oz.)	cornstarch
	37g (1⅓ oz.)	water chestnut powder (illus. 1)
	½ c.	chopped green onion
	½ c.	fresh coriander leaves

❶ Mince the lean beef and marinate in ① for one hour.

❷ Mix ② into the marinated beef. Beat the egg whites lightly (illus. 2) and add to the beef.

❸ Form the beef into balls the size of ping pong balls (illus. 3). Arrange in a steamer and steam over high heat for 8 minutes.

白菜肉捲

材料：

①	白菜葉…14片（大片完整） 絞上肉 ……150公克 香菇…4朵（泡軟切末） 竹筍丁…………⅓杯 葱花……………¼杯 紅蘿蔔絲………¼杯	②

② 香油 …………3大匙
蠔油 …………1大匙
鹽 ……………1小匙
糖……………½小匙
胡椒粉、味精 ‥少許

❶將①、②料拌勻備用。

❷白菜葉用開水燙軟、漂凉、撈起擦乾水分，硬梗用刀削薄（圖１）備用。

❸每葉白菜，包入２大匙內餡後（圖２），捲成春捲狀（圖３），入蒸籠大火蒸８分鐘即可。

Pork Cabbage Rolls

INGREDIENTS:

	14 leaves	Chinese cabbage (use large, whole leaves)
①	150g (⅓ lb.)	ground pork
	4	dried Chinese black mushrooms, soaked until soft and minced
	⅓ c.	bamboo shoots, diced
	¼ c.	chopped green onion
	¼ c.	shredded carrot
②	3 T.	sesame oil
	1 T.	oyster sauce
	1 t.	salt
	½ t.	sugar
	pinch	white pepper

❶ Mix ① and ② until well blended.

❷ Soften the cabbage leaves in boiling water, then cool in tap water. Remove from the water and wipe dry. Trim down any thick, tough stems (illus. 1).

❸ Place 2 tablespoons filling in each cabbage leaf (illus. 2), then roll into a cylindrical shape (illus. 3). Arrange in a steamer and steam over high heat for 8 minutes.

①

②

③

後記

「飲茶食譜」從民國七十九年六月初版以來，迄今三年餘，已出至第四版，肯定這本書受歡迎的程度。

就由於它廣受青睞，使我們更戰戰兢兢地針對它的內容，一再做研究。

這次，我們在四版之前，決定不惜成本修訂部分三年來日新月異研發的結果，將份量計算方面，做更精細的校對，使讀者手握此書，就能做出道地的飲茶點心。

這本書除了在台灣大為暢銷外，也在歐美、東南亞地區廣受矚目，但由於各地氣候不同，讀者在烹調時還需依當地的乾溼度酌予調整水份，其中奧妙需經幾次琢磨後，才能拿捏準確。

給您一個烹飪的概念與技巧，是我們長期掌握的方向。

Afterword

Chinese Dim Sum, since its publication in 1990, has reached the fourth edition and reaffirmed its popularity, which is also the impetus for us to continue our research in its recipes.

For the publication of fourth edition, this book was revised based on our continuous improvements over the past three years. At the same time, this resulted in more precise measurement calculations of the ingredients. By following the book, readers can easily make typical dim sum.

Besides being a best-seller in Taiwan, Chinesse Dim Sum is also receiving wide acclaims in Europe and Far East Asia. Due to the variances of weather conditions, readers should adjust the liquid used in the recipes according to the local humidity. The knack may need a few tries before reaching perfection.

To provide our readers both a skill and a perception in cooking is our goal.

Chin-Chin

5th fl., 125 Sung Chiang Rd, Taipe104 ,

純青出版社

劃撥帳號：12106299

電　話：（○二）五○七四九○二・五○八四三三一

地　址：台北市松江路125號5樓

微波食譜第一册
- 62道菜
- 112頁
- 中英對照
- 平裝280元
  精裝300元

Microwave Cooking Chinese Style
- 62 recipes
- 112 pages
- Chinese/English Bilingual

微波食譜第二册
- 76道菜
- 128頁
- 中英對照
- 平裝280元
  精裝330元

Microwave Cooking Chinese Style (II)
- 76 recipes
- 128 pages
- Chinese/English Bilingual

健康食譜
- 100道菜
- 120頁
- 中英對照
- 平裝280元

Healthful Cooking
- 100 recipes
- 120 pages
- Chinese/English Bilingual

台灣菜
- 73道菜
- 120頁
- 中英對照
- 平裝300元

Chinese Cuisine Taiwanese Style
- 73 recipes
- 120 pages
- Chinese/English Bilingual

四川菜
- 115道菜
- 96頁
- 中英對照
- 平裝300元

Chinese Cuisine Szechwan Style
- 115 recipes
- 96 pages
- Chinese/English Bilingual

上海菜
- 91道菜
- 96頁
- 中英對照
- 平裝300元

Chinese Cuisine Shanghai Style
- 91 recipes
- 96 pages
- Chinese/English Bilingual